S0-ATC-428

Crafting
NEW MEXICAN
FURNITURE

A HANDBOOK TO DESIGN, PLANS, AND TECHNIQUES ❖

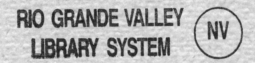
RIO GRANDE VALLEY
LIBRARY SYSTEM (NV)

Crafting
NEW MEXICAN FURNITURE

A HANDBOOK TO DESIGN, PLANS, AND TECHNIQUES

KINGSLEY H. HAMMETT

Drawings by Catherine Heller
Photography by Michael O'Shaughnessy

R·E·D
CRANE
BOOKS

1994
SANTA FE

RIO GRANDE VALLEY
LIBRARY SYSTEM

3 9075 02620531 7

This book is dedicated to my loving wife, Jerilou, who is my partner in everything I do.

Copyright © 1994 by Kingsley H. Hammett. All rights reserved. No part of this book may be reproduced in any form or by any means, including electronic or mechanical, without the expressed consent of the publisher, with the exception of brief passages embodied in critical reviews.

First Edition
Manufactured in the United States of America

Design and desktop production by John Cole Graphic Designer
Cover and text photographs by Michael O'Shaughnessy
Cover sunburst design by Ramon Martinez

Hammett, Kingsley H.
        Crafting New Mexican furniture : a handbook to design, plans, and techniques
/ Kingsley H. Hammett; drawings by Catherine Heller; photography by Michael
O'Shaughnessy. — 1st ed.
        p.   cm.
        Includes bibliographical references and index.
        ISBN 1-878610-33-3
        1. Furniture making—New Mexico —Handbooks, manuals, etc.
    I. Title.
    TT194.H35 1993
    684.1'009789—dc20   93–33987
                                                                    CIP

Red Crane Books
826 Camino de Monte Rey
Santa Fe, New Mexico 87505

ACKNOWLEDGMENTS

I want to thank Kenneth Durbrow, a Yankee craftsman in the finest tradition, who helped me build many of the pieces featured in this book; Catherine Heller, who managed to turn my scribbled sketches and scrawled numbers into professional presentations; Jim Madden, whose initial request for plans for building southwestern furniture launched this entire project; Chett Ray, who featured these plans in the Woodworker's Supply, Inc. catalog; Matt Higgins, whose suggestions led to the development of the towel racks; Joan Chernock, whose orders for custom pieces led to the development of the double bed along with the nightstand, the ropero, and the bookshelf; Olivia and Genia Lada-Mocarski, who gave me my first table saw (a 1940s vintage Delta I use to this day); Art Selzer, a renaissance tradesman who taught a fifteen-year-old the power of patience; Julie Mullen for her editing; Michael O'Shaughnessy, whose brilliant photographs enliven this book; Jim Mafchir, whose faith in the success of this project actually put it into play; and finally, Carol Caruthers, whose thorough professionalism, unflagging patience, and good humor made this project a reality.

CONTENTS

This sideboard is part of the collection
that graces the Women's Board Room
in the Museum of Fine Arts, which
opened in Santa Fe, New Mexico, in 1917.
Note the heavy chip carving and the
protruding tenons, typical of the then
popular Mission style. Museum of New
Mexico Collections, Santa Fe,
New Mexico.
Photographer: Mary Peck

This early nineteenth-century chair, which once had arms, illustrates the use of cutouts along the edges of the rails. Collection of Museum of International Folk Art, a unit of the Museum of New Mexico, Santa Fe, New Mexico. Photographer: Mary Peck

This trastero was built in Roswell, New Mexico, about 1935 and is modeled after a piece in the
Museum of New Mexico Collections. It was probably built to store clerical vestments. Permanent
Collection, Roswell Museum and Art Center, Roswell, New Mexico.

INTRODUCTION

ORIGIN OF
NEW MEXICAN STYLE

The romance of the Southwest stretches back for centuries and can be found today in New Mexico's unique style, a style which resulted from a blend of Hispanic, Native American, and Territorial influences circumscribed by available natural resources and shaped by isolation. Living in a remote outpost of the Spanish Empire for almost two and a half centuries forced settlers to produce their own necessities of everyday life. As their original pieces of ornately carved furniture wore out and disappeared, village carpenters, or *carpinteros*, replaced them with adaptations. The native versions were similar in construction, form, and decoration, yet rich with a naive frontier quality dictated by limited materials and crude tools.

The history of New Mexican furniture reflects the harsh and turbulent history of New Mexico itself. From the earliest Spanish conquistadors, to the struggling Hispanic settlers, to the conquering Yankees, to the invasion of artists, tourists, and Anglo-American archeologists, architects, and historians, the furniture of the times evolved to meet the needs and tastes of the moment. Out of this complex history has grown a unique style and tradition that continues to be practiced in every community in the state.

Spanish Colonial Period: 1598–1821

Reaching Santa Fe from Mother Spain was an arduous task in the sixteenth and seventeenth centuries. All shipments passed through Veracruz on the Gulf Coast of Mexico, were transshipped to Mexico City, and finally north up the Chihuahua trail, which was an ox-cart trip that took six months. Once it became clear to Spain that the remote Upper Rio Grande settlements held little in the way of gold and other natural riches, these far-flung northern outposts were increasingly ignored in favor of their more productive counterparts to the south.

Furniture making in this era was centered around the needs of the church, and the average settler's home had little in the way of material comforts. The wood of choice was the ponderosa pine which covered the hills and mountains on both sides of the Rio Grande valley. It was split and adzed to a workable thickness and fashioned into large pieces of furniture, no two of which were alike, held together by mortise-and-tenon joints, with square pegs and wedges to keep things tight.

Ornamentation was often employed to visually relieve the massive boards of some of their

1

weight. Spanish and Moorish motifs were carved in relief—pomegranates, rosettes, shells, lions, and scallops. Additional embellishments included heavy grooving and cutouts along table aprons and bottom rails, and hand-carved spindles and splats (ornamental bars) inspired by the window grilles popular in Spain.

Naturally, inspiration for the earliest New Mexican furniture came from pieces imported from Spain, pieces that were used, reworked, and rebuilt until nothing of the original remained. Since most settlers were too busy struggling to survive to become skilled craftsmen, their work took on an indigenous appearance. Furniture was made to meet ever-changing needs. Isolation forced new pieces to be created based only upon memories of the old designs and traditions. The new context combined with some old elements resulted in a unique style.

Most of what has survived from the earliest period are the trunks and chests used to store and ship food, household goods, and valuables. Shipping trunks that were hauled up the Chihuahua Trail were plain six-board chests with dovetailed ends reinforced by bands of iron. The more elaborate storage chests stood on legs and were strengthened by diagonal braces that ran from the front legs up to the center of the bottom rail. The legs, rails, and stiles of these chests were heavily chip-carved and their raised panels decorated with geometric patterns carved in relief. By the nineteenth century, carpenters were applying carved trim to the sides of simple five-board chests to simulate the trim and raised panels seen in the earlier chests.

The legs and aprons of tables built in this era were joined with open mortise-and-tenon joints. Aprons and stretchers were decorated with cutout designs to create "negative" space patterns, and were often separated by turned spindles or splats cut in a step design.

Similar cutout designs were made in the backs of chairs and benches, most of which were reserved for churches and homes of the wealthy. It is thought that some chairs may have been

This nineteenth-century bench shows the effects of negative space in the splats as well as the through mortise-and-tenon joinery typical of this period. Gift of the Historical Society of New Mexico. Museum of International Folk Art, Santa Fe, New Mexico.
Photographer: Mary Peck

built on Indian pueblos, judging from their deep carvings suggesting corn stalks, rain, and the heavens. *Trasteros*, or cupboards, had doors that swung on pintel hinges. Crests, cut into the shape of fans or scallops, often adorned the top fronts and sides of such pieces and were held there by dados cut in the legs which extended above the top of the cabinets.

Anglo-American Period: 1821–1900

Up until 1821, all commerce between New Mexico and the outside world was controlled by the Spanish Crown and contact with travelers from the East was banned. That changed when William Becknell headed west from Franklin, Missouri, loaded with goods to trade with the Native Americans. At the territory's border he learned of Mexico's newly won independence from Spain. He pushed on to Santa Fe where he turned a handsome profit, thus opening the Santa Fe Trail. Records show that after inexpensive textiles, the most sought after goods in Santa Fe Trail trade were hardware and tools, the most significant being the frame saw and molding planes.

As more easterners came into the new territory, the army followed, and in 1847 Brigadier General Stephen Watts Kearny raised the Stars and Stripes above an adobe building on the plaza in Las Vegas and declared the territory part of the United States. Fort Union was established several miles north on the Santa Fe Trail and at its peak employed one thousand artisans to build and maintain the wagons, wheels, and weapons necessary to a nineteenth-century fighting force, bringing sorely needed modern technology to the New Mexico Territory.

That same year, the army built the first New Mexico sawmill in Santa Fe, and soon sawn planks were readily available throughout the area. For the next half century the cabinet and furniture trades were dominated by European-born craftsmen who brought with them the Empire style so popular in the East. Their clients were mostly Hispanics growing prosperous on the new trade with the East and the German-Jewish and Anglo-American families lured West by this new commerce. To meet the demands of the new taste, their output included furniture forms that had not yet entered the Hispanic vocabulary— chests of drawers, bookcases, wash stands, and writing desks.

On New Year's Day, 1879, the railroad made its debut in Las Vegas and pushed from there on to Albuquerque and west to Los Angeles and

This heavily chip-carved chest from the nineteenth century has diagonal braces set into the legs and bottom rail to help keep the chest square when the wood shrinks. Spanish Colonial Arts Society, Inc. Collection on loan to the Museum of International Folk Art, a unit of the Museum of New Mexico, Santa Fe, New Mexico.
Photographer: Mary Peck

San Diego. New Mexico now found itself firmly rooted on the transcontinental transportation grid, and furniture mass produced on the East Coast that was once brought over the Santa Fe Trail by the wagonload was now brought into the territory by the rail carload. That made it more affordable, and consequently popular among the more sophisticated families throughout New Mexico.

Still well removed from the centers of commerce, craftsmen at work in the isolated villages of northern New Mexico from the mid-1860s to the mid-1890s were inspired by the new tools and stylistic influences. They developed their own charming, vernacular style in which traditional pieces were decorated with intricate cutouts, turnings, and applied wood panels reminiscent of the Empire, Greek Revival, Mission, and Craftsman styles popular at that time.

The arrival of the frame saw allowed carpenters to express their handiwork with applied panels on chests clearly inspired by the gingerbread house trim popular on homes being built at the time. Sometimes these appliques were little more than reeded diamonds and other geometric shapes. Bed and chair legs took on a decided Empire curve, while their backs were made from more finely turned, plain, tapered spindles. *Trasteros* became wardrobes under the Anglo-American influence and were topped with crown moldings. Some were highly painted and "grained," while others sported punched tin fronts reminiscent of the Hoosier cabinets of the Midwest.

Revival Period: 1920–Present

The railroad brought a flood of new visitors from the East, captivated by the romanticism of the West and particularly by the Indian cultures. Santa Fe found a new economic base in this tourism, which led in turn to its development as an art center and a mecca for those interested in archaeology, anthropology, and the collecting of traditional Hispanic and Indian crafts.

New Mexican furniture making, which had fallen into idleness during the first twenty years of the twentieth century as the needs of the locals were met by factory-produced imports, was revived with the new state's participation in the California-Panama Exposition in San Diego in 1915. Here the architectural firm of Rapp and Rapp built a Pueblo-style building and the Santa Fe Railroad sponsored a Painted Desert exhibit. Two years later, Rapp and Rapp used the same ideas from the San Diego exposition—the soft, rounded curves of adobe, levels that stepped up in seemingly random patterns, and roof beams of peeled pine logs that protruded through the exterior walls—to design and build the Fine Arts Museum on the northwest corner of the Santa Fe Plaza. In 1921, Isaac Hamilton Rapp designed the La Fonda Hotel, a Santa Fe landmark which became a signature for the new Santa Fe style.

The style was a mixture of Spanish colonial and Pueblo Indian elements. The designs carved

This desk, made in Taos for Roy, New Mexico, sheep farmer Mariano Chavez about 1890, shows the Anglo-American influence of the Eastlake style then popular on the East Coast. The window in the door is fashioned from a discarded washboard and the molding is nailed to the piece for added decoration. Collection of the Mariano Chavez Family, Santa Fe, New Mexico.
Photographer: Mary Peck

into the massive beams and corbels in the new museum were adapted from drawings made at historic sites up and down the Rio Grande. Similar themes, including chip carving painted in dull reds and blues and protruding tenons adapted from the Mission and Craftsman styles, found their way into the furniture built for the museum's Women's Board Room and became signatures of the Spanish Revival period from the 1940s until today.

Wealthy Anglo-Americans, many drawn to Santa Fe to take the cure for tuberculosis, got caught up in the preservation movement and in 1922 formed a committee to restore the old mission churches. Several painters began making, carving, and painting furniture, and in the process stretched the definition of New Mexican style to new limits. During this period, these same wealthy patrons and American and European artists started collecting antique New Mexico furniture, carved beams, and doors. They incorporated these fixtures into newly built and remodeled older adobe homes which they further decorated with Hispanic religious carvings and paintings along with weavings and tinwork. This intense interest in Spanish arts and crafts led directly to the handicraft revival of the 1930s.

In 1925, Mary Austin and Frank Applegate formed the Society for the Revival of Spanish Colonial Arts, which was renamed the Spanish Colonial Arts Society in 1929. Members collected work which they intended to serve as models for new craftsmen and hosted Hispanic craft shows during the annual fiestas in Santa Fe. The society also operated a retail store in Santa Fe's Sena Plaza from 1930 to 1933, providing furniture makers and craftsmen with a local outlet.

When the Great Depression led to the collapse of New Mexico's rural subsistence economy, Brice Sewell, state director of vocational education, came to the aid of the struggling Hispanic villages with vocational education programs. By pooling funds obtained through the Works Progress Administration, the National Youth Administration, the Federal Relief Administration, the Civilian Conservation Corps, and the Emergency Education Program, among others, Sewell created furniture-making programs across the state, beginning with pilot projects in Santa Fe, Rio Arriba, and Taos counties. These programs emphasized using local resources to create saleable products, and taught native New Mexicans business management and sales skills. The furniture programs provided finished pieces for the Spanish Arts Shop and Native Market stores in Santa Fe and contracted to furnish many public buildings around the state.

Eventually, Sewell managed to create craft centers in more than forty different towns across New Mexico. These WPA facilities functioned more as community centers than just training schools, and gave rise to a new look in New Mexican furniture, thereafter referred to as WPA

This chair is part of a set built by a local carpenter for the Albuquerque Community Theater in the 1930s. Collection of the Albuquerque Community Theater, Albuquerque, New Mexico. Photographer: Mary Peck

style. Sewell's organization published a booklet, known as the Blue Book, which laid out acceptable design standards for traditional eighteenth- and nineteenth-century-style furniture designs. It was written and illustrated by Bill Lumpkins, a woodworker and architectural draftsman who became a teacher's trainer. Copies of the book are still used sixty years later in many New Mexican cabinet shops.

As the war in Europe created work in defense factories by the late 1930s, as many as half the men and boys of working age left the villages of New Mexico for the shipyards and aircraft factories of California and employed their woodworking skills as pattern makers.

After World War II, and again following the close of the Korean conflict, statewide vocational programs once more offered furniture making to returning veterans, many of which were taught by *carpinteros* who had honed their skills in the WPA centers. Today, their children and grandchildren, including George Sandoval and his son Chris Manzanares Sandoval of Albuquerque, David E. C'deBaca and Miguel Chaves of Santa Fe, and Roberto Lavadie and Laz Cardeñas of Taos, proudly carry the traditions forward in the company of a new infusion of craftspeople.

Today, furniture making is a thriving industry throughout New Mexico. Furniture companies currently active number somewhere between five hundred and one thousand. Many are independent craftspeople operating in out-

Pieces like this bed, built during the Revival period, often employed open mortise-and-tenon joints. Their tenons and locking pegs jutted past the legs. This technique was made popular at the time by builders of Mission-style furniture. Collection of the School of American Research, Santa Fe, New Mexico.
Photographer: Mary Peck

Some are adopted directly from historical pieces I have come across, while others are original creations that use some of the more common design elements to give them a New Mexican flavor. I hope they will inspire you, as the original designs from which they were drawn inspired me.

Why Me?

I can't swear to it from a distance of four decades, but I probably grew up with one of those toys where you pound colored pegs into holes with a wooden mallet. It seems I've had a hammer in my hand most of my life, although I have earned a good deal of my living doing other things. Woodworking has given me endless hours of entertainment and satisfaction, and I am delighted to have the opportunity to pass along some of what I have learned.

When I set out to make my first piece of furniture as a twenty-six-year-old newlywed, I asked an elderly friend if I could come to his house to see what he had built and how he had built it. He told me that he began building his own furniture as a young man when his desire for a certain piece outweighed his ability to buy it. I realized that was also my motivation.

I wasn't exactly new to the woodworking world at that point. In the early 1950s we lived in a suburban New Jersey development. As a grade school student, my interest in playing football and baseball was matched only by the insatiable joy I found watching workmen build houses down the street. On trips to New York City I would peep through openings in plywood barricades at the fascinating construction

of-the-way locations in small, home-based shops, while some larger firms employ up to sixty workers. In recent years, their style has been copied, carried to neighboring states, and renamed Southwest style. But the authentic look from which all these replicas derived was developed in New Mexico almost four hundred years ago.

Why This Book?

When I moved to New Mexico and wanted to build some pieces in the Southwest tradition, I was surprised at the lack of readily available information. I bought the few books that dealt with New Mexican furniture, but none of them gave me the designs and details I was looking for. So, I developed the designs in this book from my own observations, adapting traditional elements to contemporary uses.

These plans are intended to serve as a guide to building furniture in the New Mexican tradition, but they are not offered as rigid formulas for building pieces as drawn or as photographed.

that took place deep in muddy holes beside Manhattan streets. And when my father built a summer house of his own design, I was allowed, at the age of eight or so, to actually bang in some nails to hold down the Masonite subfloor.

Every afternoon after school I would drag bits and pieces of plywood, 2x4s, and bent nails to my backyard from nearby housing developments. I straightened the nails, cut the wood with a hand saw, and set to building quite a substantial clubhouse, complete with a built-in ladder and removable hatch to get up on the roof. But simply sitting in the completed clubhouse wasn't much fun, so I tore it down and built another, larger one.

My parents recognized my fascination with tools and wood, and they knew about my desire to build things. They sent me to the home of a gentleman who offered a Saturday morning carpentry class. The summer I was fourteen I worked for Art Selzer, who took care of a big house, a large motor yacht, and a smaller runabout for a wealthy oil tycoon. When the day was done, he helped me design and build different things. The most notable and durable turned out to be a pair of rudders for a catamaran and a set of hatch screens for a friend's family sailboat. Many years later both were still in hard use, a testament to the patience and concentration I learned from Art.

I went on to become the president of the woodworking club in high school, but did not

The sweeping curve of the legs on this late nineteenth-century side chair shows the influence of the Empire style on New Mexico furniture making. Collection of Dr. and Mrs. Ward Alan Minge, Corrales, New Mexico.
Photographer: Mary Peck

do very much woodworking after that until I found myself married and in need of some furniture. Slowly my skills came back, and I spent the next twenty years in and out of the construction and furniture making businesses.

My need for furniture arose again many years later, when I moved from the East Coast to New Mexico. In Santa Fe, the furniture making tradition went back four hundred years, and soon I found that I was swept up in its mystery.

I started out by making a table, which I later traded in the time-honored Santa Fe tradition to an artist friend for a beautiful painting I later sold for $1,500. Not bad for a project cobbled together in a friend's backyard with little more than the construction tools I always carried in my van.

When I needed a bed, I got some old beams from an abandoned coal mine south of Santa Fe, dragged them to a local lumber mill, and got them sliced into planks. I fashioned a beautiful bed where the red of the sixty-year-old pine contrasted with the blackened streaks of coal dust embedded in the beams. I later traded that bed to the same artist friend for another painting that I later traded for the computer on which I am writing this book.

My step-daughter's bed was next; a single bed I made from alder carved with three hearts across the headboard. Then, I built another queen bed to replace the one we had traded to our artist friend. Projects for other friends followed. Many were traded for fine works of art, while others were sold outright to paying customers. Eventually, as an offshoot of work I was doing in small-scale economic development, I formed the New Mexico Wood Products Association and went on to publish the New Mexico Furniture Catalog, the New Mexico Supply Catalog, the New Mexico Whole House Catalog, the New Mexico Home Catalog, and the Lifestyle New Mexico Catalog. By then I had a brochure of different bed designs and a notebook filled with photographs of tables I had built and other ideas gleaned from magazines and newspapers.

In the summer of 1992, the new products manager at Woodworker's Supply, Inc., one of the largest mail order tool supply companies in the country, asked me to develop plans for some southwestern pieces in response to the many inquiries the company had received. I teamed up with illustrator Catherine Heller, and we developed a set of plans for three beds. Next came plans for the tables, nightstand, bookshelf, and *ropero.* They all sold well, and we expanded the

This small stand was probably made in the Peñasco area of northern New Mexico in the late nineteenth or early twentieth century. It has molding nailed to the door to make it look like framing. Collection of Mr. and Mrs. Larry Frank, Arroyo Hondo, New Mexico.
Photographer : Mary Peck

collection by adding a line of smaller, easier-to-build projects like the *repisas,* the hat and towel racks, the four boxes, and the blanket chests.

I have had a wonderful time building all these pieces, and, judging by the number of single plans we have sold so far, so have many hundreds of other woodworkers. I hope you find here the inspiration you are looking for, and I encourage you to adapt anything in this book to your own needs. Feel free to add or delete your own decorative patterns, as did the revivalist furniture makers of the 1930s, add or delete details and embellishments, use joinery with which you are comfortable, and change any dimensions to fit your own space needs. Experiment and improvise to suit your own taste. But above all, HAVE FUN!

Kingsley Hammett
Santa Fe, New Mexico

OVERVIEW

BUILDING IN THE SOUTHWEST STYLE

*U*p until the twentieth century, *carpinteros* in isolated villages of northern New Mexico built the furniture they needed much as I built my first pieces in Santa Fe. They applied simple hand tools to readily available materials, adapting familiar designs to meet specific needs. Their designs were originally influenced by furniture shipped from Spain and carted up from the Mexican interior along the Camino Real. Over the generations, however, as the original pieces wore out and Spain's influence waned, the designs took on a distinctly indigenous New Mexican flavor.

TOOLS

The *carpinteros* of the Spanish colonies didn't have much in the way of fine woodworking tools. They felled ponderosa pines on the slopes of the Sangre de Cristo Mountains, split them into crude planks, and thinned them down to a workable thickness with an adz. Using only a crude *serrucho*, or saw, they cut their planks to length based on the *vara*, the Spanish unit of measurement roughly equivalent to our yard. Their work was fastened together with through mortise-and-tenon joints held tight with wooden pegs and wedges, and they decorated their pieces with carvings made by using flat chisels and concave gouges.

Despite the limited tools, the resulting furniture was quite lovely and well proportioned. Fortunately, modern technology has relieved us of the vast toil it took to fashion a piece and we can now re-create furniture in the New Mexican style with a minimum of effort.

Hand Tools

To make any of the pieces shown in this book, your hand tool collection should include these basic items:

- ❖ set of flat chisels (¼", ½", and ¾")
- ❖ compass
- ❖ v-groove gouge
- ❖ wooden mallet
- ❖ claw hammer
- ❖ back saw
- ❖ steel tape measure
- ❖ steel yardstick
- ❖ sliding T-square
- ❖ sliding bevel
- ❖ framing square
- ❖ try square
- ❖ #3 Phillips-head screwdriver
- ❖ block plane
- ❖ Dowel-It jig (allows you to drill various sized holes exactly centered in a piece of stock)

- two 12" bar clamps
- six ¾", 4' long pipe bar clamps (threaded both ends so two can be combined to make two 8' clamps)
- index of twist and Forstner bits

Portable Power Tools

While the *carpinteros* who built furniture in New Mexico for the first three hundred years did not have power tools at their disposal, we do and I'm in favor of using them:

- ⅜" drill
- ¼ sheet palm sander
- 6" random orbital sander
- belt sander
- saber saw
- router(s) with ⅜" bullnose, chamfer, ¼" and ⅝" straight cuts, ½" x ⅞" 14-degree dovetail, and v-groove bits
- circular saw

Stationary Power Tools

You can build everything in this book with the basic hand tools and portable power tools, but your work will be more accurate if you also use the following stationary tools:

- 6" jointer
- 10" table saw
- 10" radial arm saw
- three-bead molding cutter
- set of 6" dado cutters

The following aren't absolutely necessary, but are very handy to have:

- 14" band saw
- 10" planer
- sixteen-speed floor-model drill press with mortise attachment

MATERIALS

Woods

New Mexican furniture is generally built of pine, which has both advantages and drawbacks. Ponderosa is native to the state, and is generally a tougher wood than, say, sugar pine, which is sweeter smelling, lighter, and easier to work. However, sugar pine is also very soft and dents easily.

Ponderosa is often found with beautiful red streaks, and the grades below clear come with knots, most of which are tight. Sometimes, however, a knot will be surrounded by growth rings and it can leave a gap if you cut into and loosen it. You can ease any sharp edges with a block plane and/or flat chisel, but you don't need to sand out all the rough marks. Don't worry if a chip is left in the side of a table leg, for example. These marks will give the finished piece an air of authenticity and signal that it was built by a real human being. That's woodworking New Mexican style. I have also had some luck with inexpensive Idaho white pine. But, as the name suggests, it is very white and doesn't have the natural red beauty of ponderosa.

Sometimes I use hardwood dowels to give my tables a handcrafted look.

Finishes

I finish all my pieces with a coat of natural pine-colored stain, and then, because my wife is sensitive to strong odors of any kind, I go back over the stain with a coat or two of clear water-based sealer. That too has its own lingering aroma, so I wind up with a light coat of natural beeswax. Both the non-toxic stain and beeswax are available from Natural Choice, 1365 Rufina Circle, Santa Fe, NM 87501, (505) 438-3448. The non-toxic sealers can be ordered from AFM Enterprises, 2405 Maclovia Lane, Santa Fe, NM 87501, (505) 471-4549.

When it comes to painting the chests, do as the *carpinteros* do; use whatever colors are left on your shelf.

Hardware

Use wood glue and 4d finish nails in assembling these pieces, and standard sheetrock screws when fastening ledgers to the bottoms of chests, *roperos,* and bookshelves.

Bed rail fasteners are available at any good hardware store or may be ordered from Woodworker's Supply, Inc., 5604 Alameda Place NE, Albuquerque, NM 87501, (800) 645-9292. They are made of cast iron and allow you to create a good, fast connection between bed rails and the legs of a headboard or footboard.

Decorative wrought iron hinges are not easy to find. One source for ironwork made in Mexico is Santa Fe Doors, 3615 High St. NE, Albuquerque, NM 87107, (505) 345-3160. Send them a photo or drawing of what you need, and they will have it made. A second source is Dimestore Cowboys, 4500 Hawkins NE, Albuquerque, NM 87109, (505) 345-3933.

Large-size reprints of the plans offered in this book are available for $8 each from Fine Additions, Inc., 2405 Maclovia Lane, Santa Fe, NM 87501, (505) 471-4549.

DESIGN DETAILS AND EMBELLISHMENTS

To relieve the blank mass of the pine planks used in traditional New Mexican furniture, *carpinteros* developed a number of different design details. Some have their roots in the sacred symbolism of Spain and Europe, while others are drawn from the striking New Mexico landscape and Native American culture. I use many of them in the pieces featured in this book. Here is how I make each one. (These examples are intended for general reference. Details and dimensions will vary with each piece you make.)

Sunburst

The sunburst is one of my favorite designs. It is adapted from the rosette design, a scallop shell motif popular in the time of the Renaissance. In

Sunburst

Rosette

more or less the same way. I use the following method.

Start by drawing a vertical line down the center of the piece. Next, draw three horizontal lines (about two inches apart, for a headboard) starting at the top. Divide each vertical half of the piece into three or four equal sections, depending upon how many arcs you want to end up with. Then, scribe arcs between the descending points, using anything that has a pleasing curve (like a trash can lid for a headboard or a small bottle cap for a small corner rosette).

Next, draw straight lines from the point at the bottom center of the headboard out to the points where the arcs intersect. Cut the arcs with a saber saw and the straight lines with a v-shaped router bit. Go over the routed lines with a straight chisel to give the grooves a hand-cut look, and route a bullnose along the top of the headboard.

To draw arcs bigger than any circular form conveniently available, I use a technique borrowed from the world of boat building. Tack small finish nails at the points where the vertical and horizontal lines intersect, then hold a thin batten between any two points, pull it upward into a pleasing curve, and scribe it with a pencil.

ancient Spain, the rosette symbolized one's Christianity and allegiance to the faith. According to Sali Katz, author of *Hispanic Furniture,* the shell represents San Diego, or Saint James, the patron saint of Spain, whose name inspired the cry "Santiago" as the Christians overwhelmed the Moors in the fifteenth century. The shell also symbolizes birth and resurrection.

The rosette detail became popular during the New Mexican furniture revival spurred by the Works Progress Administration in the 1930s and 1940s. It is frequently seen in full form as a circle or oval, in half form as a sunburst, or in quarters to decorate the corners of boxes and trunks. Rosettes are either carved down into the forgiving pine or left standing in relief.

I seldom create the same sunburst twice, as the design and dimensions vary with each piece. In each case, however, the outline is drawn in

12

Beads, Grooves, and Kerfs

Colonial *carpinteros* were always partial to beads and grooves, which became easier to make after decorative block planes made their way into the New Mexico territory with the opening of the Santa Fe Trail. Many historical museum pieces use the three-bead design.

I use a three-bead cutter in my table saw and generally cut lines along the top and bottom edges of my table aprons. A similar effect can be achieved by running the piece over the table saw blade set to cut no more than one-eighth to one-quarter inch deep. Cut as many (or as few) parallel lines as you like. Setting the fence closer to the three-bead cutter lets you cut a single bead down the outside of a leg.

Beads and Grooves

Steps

Steps

The step design is a popular element adopted from the Native American culture. The geometric corners suggest the profile of a typical pueblo dwelling as well as the outlines of the surrounding mountains and mesas.

To cut a step design into the pieces of what will become a table apron, for example, clamp the two pieces together, and lay out the design on the front face and along the tops. If the pieces are not too wide, put dado cutters in the radial arm saw and remove the material down to the lines of the desired pattern. Larger pieces can be cut with a saber saw or on a band saw.

13

Negative Space

Beautiful effects can be achieved through the use of negative space, the pattern that remains after material is removed. Creating a stepped negative space is done in a manner similar to cutting the step design, only in this case, begin by taking the pieces in which the pattern will appear and ripping them in two. Turn the new pieces so the edges just ripped are facing upward. Clamp together as many as feasible and lay out the pattern on the front face and along the tops. Mark the right hand edges so you know how deep to make your cuts. Remove the material with the dado cutters in the radial arm saw, beginning with the deepest cut first, then raise the saw blade in increments to do the shallower cuts. Put the sets of halves back together; the light shining through will outline your cutout pattern.

Patterns with less regular edges, like the gull wing and diamond patterns, may be cut on a band saw.

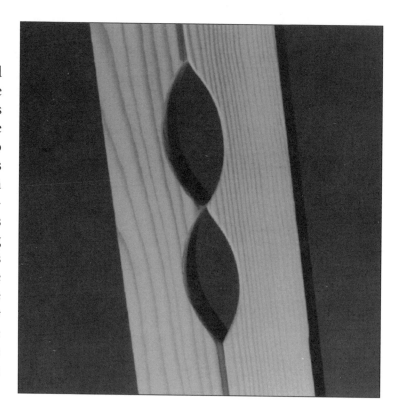

Gull Wing Pattern Cutout

Step Pattern Cutout

Diamond Pattern Cutout

Scallops

Scallops

To cut a scallop outline, strike parallel lines about three inches apart from one end of the work piece to the other. Hold a jar top or other arc tangent to the vertical lines and the top of the work piece and scribe the curves. Cut the pattern with a saber saw or on a band saw.

15

Applique

Colonial *carpinteros* often decorated the surface panels of chests with cutout designs like the four shown in the section on Blanket Chests. Cut them out on a band saw, relieve the edges with a sharp chisel, then nail and glue them to the outside of the box.

Bullets and Chip Carving

Bullets and chip carving are two other popular traditional design embellishments. While I did not employ them on the pieces in this book, they are appropriate when decorating almost any flat surface. Both can be used in infinite geometric configurations.

Bullets

Cutting Parallel Lines with Sheetrock Knife (Utility Knife)

Bullets are created with gouges of varying sizes. Lay out a pattern, and, with the concave face of the gouge toward your right, begin carving the bullet by cutting into the stock with one vertical downward blow. Then move the gouge about one inch to the right and come back to the left with a series of softer blows, cutting downward until you meet the first cut. When the chip is removed, the hollowed out space resembles the profile of a bullet.

Chip carving can be done using flat chisels to create many different patterns. One popular design is to cut two parallel lines ¾ inch apart with a sheetrock knife. Divide the band into 1-inch increments. Using a ¾-inch chisel, cut downward from the first perpendicular line halfway to the next perpendicular line, and so on until you reach the end of the stock. Turn the

16

piece end for end, and repeat the process, removing the shallow v-shaped pieces as you go. The end result will resemble a basket weave, particularly when one facet is painted one color and the opposing facet a different, contrasting color. (Red and blue is one very traditional combination.)

Removing Chips with Chisel

V-groove

V-grooves

Strike four blows with a v-groove gouge to create a cross, a star, or a compass rose.

JOINTS

The most popular joint in traditional New Mexican furniture was the overlapping through mortise-and-tenon, reinforced with a peg for maximum strength and holding power. The following is a list of joints used in the designs in this book.

Edge Joints

To join a series of narrower boards together into a larger one; to build a table top, for example, use one of the following joints:

Butt—The boards are edge-glued together.

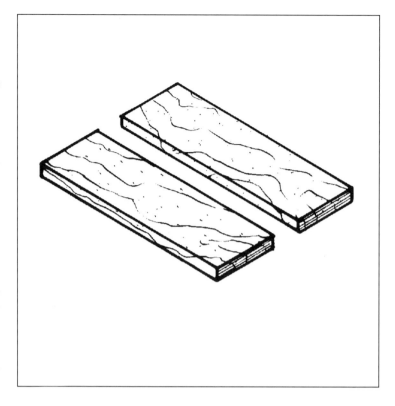

Butt Joint

Dowel Joint

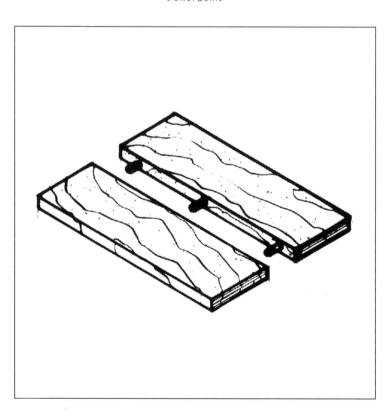

Dowel—The edges are edge-glued together with a series of dowels in between.

Corner and Angle Joints

To join a vertical board to a horizontal board; to join the edge of a shelf to its back, for example, use one of the following joints:

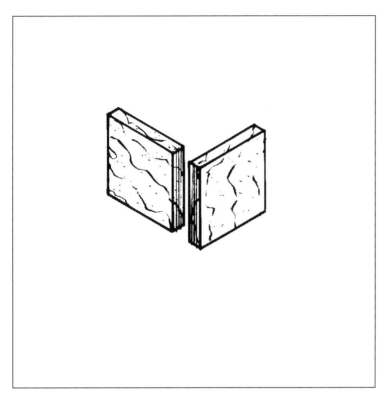

Butt Joint

Butt—The side of the edge of one board rests on the edge face of the other.

Rabbet Joint

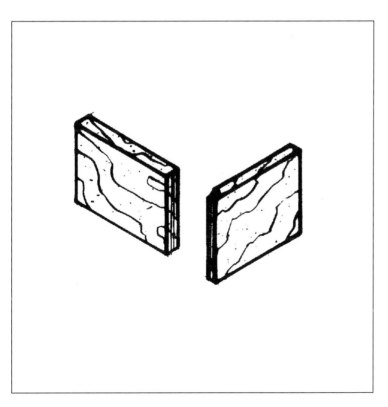

Rabbet—A slot is cut in the side of the edge of one board to accept the thickness of the other board.

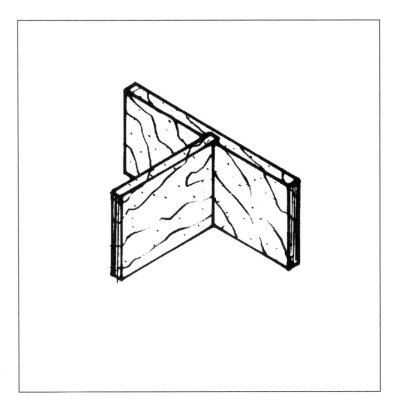

Dado—A slot is cut in one board to accept the thickness of the other.

Dado Joint

Blind Mortise-and-Tenon Joint

Mortise-and-Tenon Joints

A tenon (tongue) is cut into one board and a matching mortise (hole) is cut into the other. Following are several variations on this basic joint:

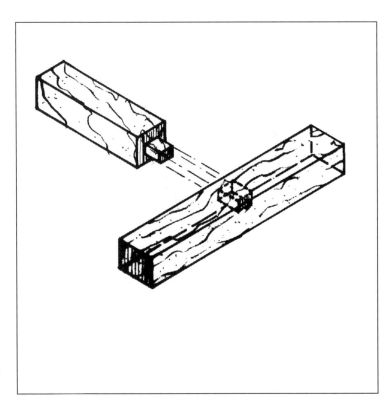

Blind—The tenon does not penetrate the mating piece.

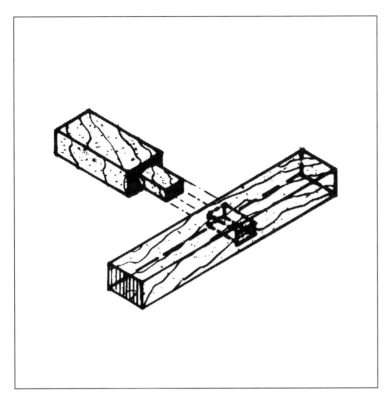

Through Mortise-and-Tenon Joint

Through—The tenon penetrates the mating piece.

Open Mortise-and-Tenon Joint

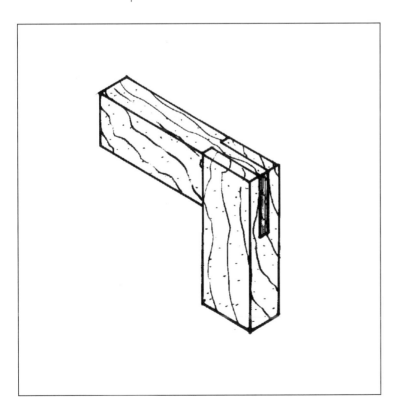

Open—The tenon slides down into the mortise from the top.

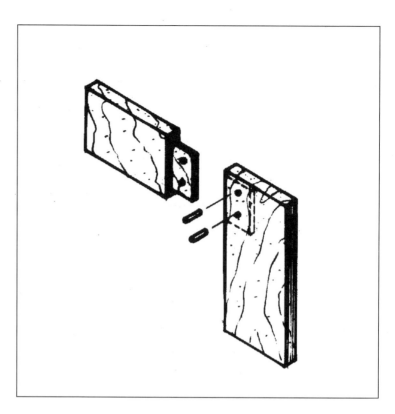

Stub—The joint is blind, and the tenon is relatively short.

Stub Mortise-and-Tenon Joint

Dovetail Joint

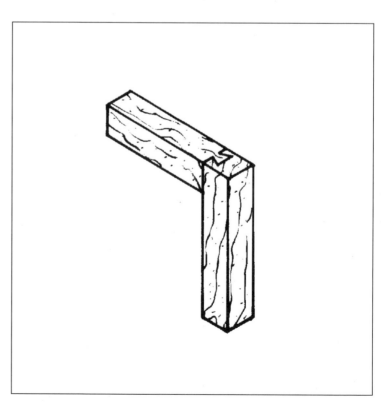

Dovetail—The tenon slides down into the mortise from the top. This can be cut with a dovetail router bit.

Trash Box

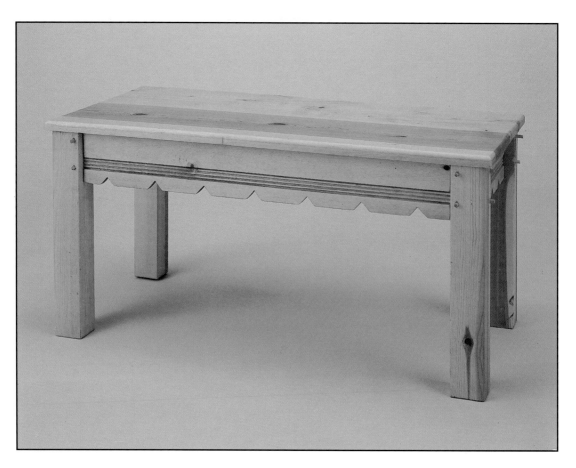

Coffee Table

Rectangular Footstool

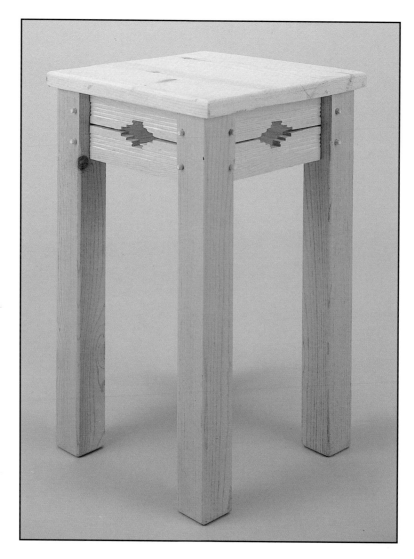

End Table

Square Footstool

Eight-square Chest

Cross Chest

Step Chest

BOXES

Here are designs for four boxes—a clothes hamper, a newspaper recycling box, a trash box, and a wastepaper box—that are easy and fun to make and require only the simplest of woodworking skills and tools. All of these boxes are assembled with simple butt joints.

CLOTHES HAMPER

Design

The illustration on page 33 depicts the finished hamper with a hinged, slanted lid. The negative space cutouts are useful here, allowing air to circulate to the clothes within, while on the other designs they are used for decoration only.

Creating the Cutouts

Clamp the front and side pieces together (there are no cutouts in the back panel) and lay out the negative space pattern shown at right in pencil on the front face. Remove the material on a radial arm saw or with a saber saw. Put the panel pieces back together with a little spot of glue and clamp them up for a time where they meet.

Building the Box

CREATING THE SLANT

Along the top edge of each side panel, measure 5¾ inches in from the back and mark the spot. Then mark a spot 23 inches up the front edge of each side panel. Draw a line on the outside of each side panel connecting the two points, and cut along that line.

Set the blade on the table or radial arm saw to the angle of the slanted portion of the side panel top, and cut a matching bevel along the top edge of the front piece so the slanted top will rest on it smoothly.

ASSEMBLING THE BOX WALLS

Using 4d finish nails, nail the front panel onto the front edges of the two side panels. Then nail the back panel onto the back edges of the two side panels.

PUTTING THE BOTTOM IN PLACE

Glue and screw a ledger around the inside of the four walls of the box, about 1 inch up from the bottom. (A ledger is simply a piece of 1-inch-square stock upon which the bottom rests and through which screws can hold the bottom in place. Where appropriate, a ledger may also be used to secure a top, as in the case of a table or nightstand, to the piece's frame.) Place bottom panels inside the box and fit them into place so they are resting on the ledger strips. Then drive 1¼-inch sheetrock screws up through the bottom of the ledger strips into the underside of the bottom panels to hold them in place.

Fabricating the Hamper Top

Cut a 5¾-inch strip off the back edge of the top panel. Glue and nail it with 4d finish nails so it rests on the top edge of the back panel and along the backs of the top edges of the side panels. Bevel the back edge of the loose top panel so it meets the front edge of the fixed top panel smoothly.

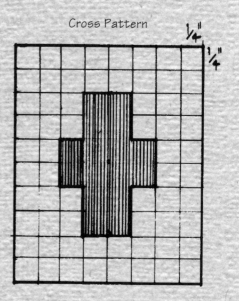

Cross Pattern
¼"
¼"

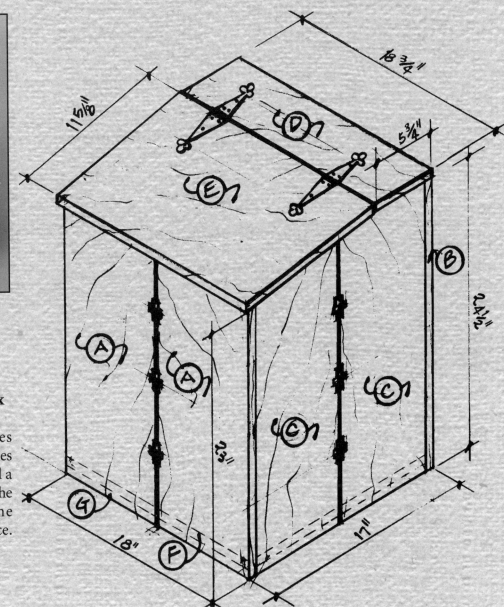

Fastening the Top to the Box

Hand-forged strap hinges from Mexico, set about 3 inches in from the outside edges, add a nice touch to this hamper. See the Hardware heading in the Overview section for a source.

CUTTING LIST

Clothes Hamper
(18" x 17" x 24 1/2")

Part	Qty	T	W	L	Piece
A	2	¾"	9"	23"	Front
B	2	¾"	9"	24½"	Back
C	4	¾"	7¾"	24½"	Sides
D	1	¾"	5¾"	18¾"	Fixed Top
E	1	¾"	11⅝"	18¾"	Hinged Top
F	1	¾"	16½"	15½"	Bottom
G	1	¾"	¾"	to fit	Ledger Material

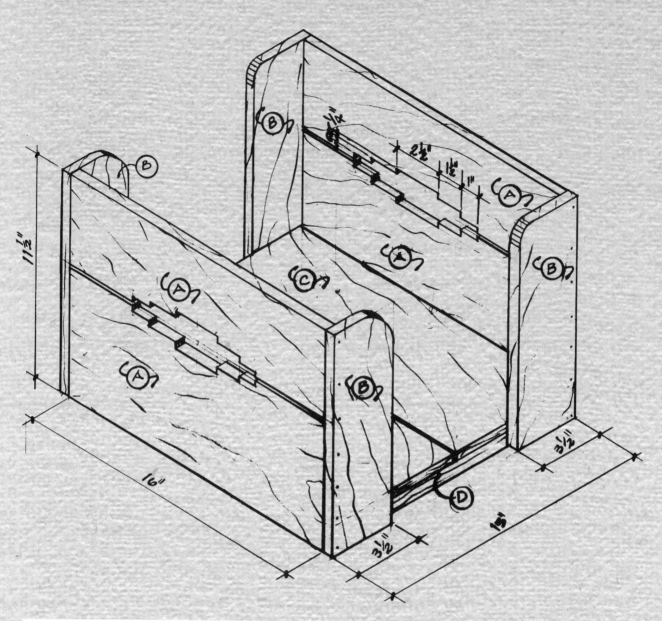

CUTTING LIST

Newspaper Recycling Box
(16" x 15" x 11½")

Part	Qty	T	W	L	Piece
A	4	¾"	5¾"	16"	Sides
B	4	¾"	3½"	11½"	Ends
C	2	¾"	6¾"	16"	Bottom
D	1	¾"	¾"	to fit	Ledger Material

NEWSPAPER RECYCLING BOX

Design

Everyone, it seems, is collecting newspapers to recycle these days. You can buy a plastic recycling box in any discount store, or you can toss them into a paper carton out in the garage until recycling day. But here is an attractive southwestern style box (see the illustration on page 34) that is nice to have near your favorite reading chair to collect newspapers until it's their time to go.

Creating the Cutouts

Clamp the four side pieces together, lay out your negative space pattern along the front and top of the clamped-together stack, and remove the material with the radial arm saw or saber saw. Glue the panels with the cutouts back together, edge to edge.

Clamp the four end pieces together and mark a rounded corner on one top corner (a 1-gallon can yields a nice curve). Cut along the line with a band saw or saber saw.

Building the Box

MAKING THE BOTTOM

Make the bottom by gluing and nailing four pieces of ledger material along the bottoms of the outside edges of the bottom panels.

Assembling the Box

To assemble the box, nail the side pieces to the side edges of the bottom pieces, and then nail the four end pieces to both the sides and the bottom.

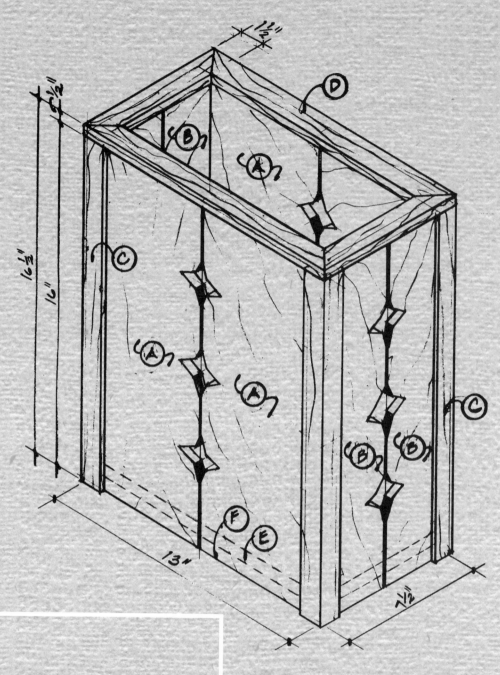

CUTTING LIST

Trash Box
(13" x 7½" x 16½")

Part	Qty	T	W	L	Piece
A	4	¾"	6½"	16"	Front/Back
B	4	¾"	3¾"	16"	Ends
C	1	¾"	¾"	64"	Corner Molding
D	1	¾"	1½"	to fit	Lattice
E	1	¾"	¾"	to fit	Ledger Material
F	1	¾"	6"	11½"	Bottom

Star Pattern

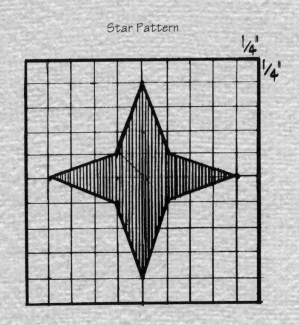

1/4" 1/4"

TRASH BOX

Design

This trash box (see the illustration on page 36) is designed so its interior dimensions match those of the typical brown paper grocery bag.

Creating the Cutouts

Clamp the four side pieces together and the four end pieces together and lay out the star pattern as shown above. Cut away the waste on a band saw or with a radial arm saw.

Glue and clamp the pieces together edge to edge, so you're working with just two sides and two ends.

Building the Box

ASSEMBLING THE BOX WALLS

Glue and nail the side panels onto the edges of the end panels. Nail a ¾-inch corner molding over the corners where the sides and end panels come together. Nail pieces of lattice material to the four top edges, with the corners cut to meet at 45-degree angles.

PUTTING THE BOTTOM IN PLACE

Screw a ledger around the inside of the four walls, about 1 inch up from the bottom edge. Place the bottom panel inside the box and fit it into place on the ledger. Drive screws up through the bottom of the ledger into the bottom panel to hold it in place.

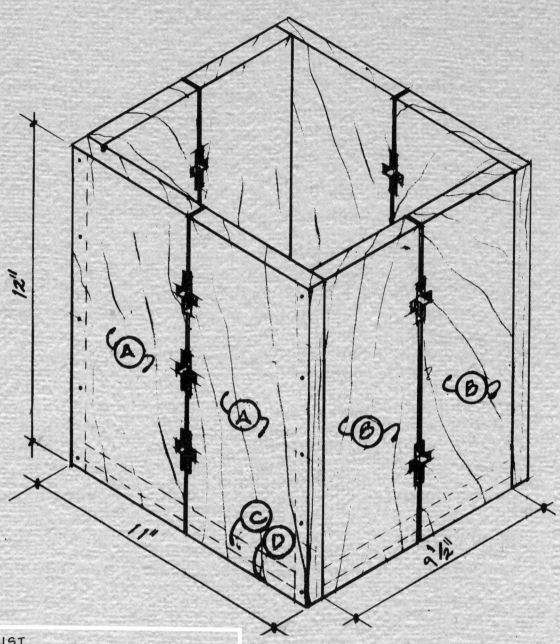

CUTTING LIST

Wastepaper Box
(11" x 11" x 12")

Part	Qty	T	W	L	Piece
A	4	¾"	5½"	12"	Front/Back
B	4	¾"	4¾"	12"	Ends
C	1	¾"	¾"	to fit	Ledger Material
D	1	¾"	9½"	9½"	Bottom

WASTEPAPER BOX

Design

This little wastepaper box (see the illustration on page 38) is simply a smaller version of the trash box, without the extra corner molding or top edge trim.

Creating the Cutouts

Stack and clamp the four sides together and the four ends together. Lay out the negative space pattern on both the front boards and along the tops of the stacks, and remove the waste with dado cutters on a radial arm saw. Make three cutouts on the sides and two on the ends. Glue and clamp the cut out edges of the pieces back together to form two sides and two ends.

Building the Box

ASSEMBLING THE BOX
WALLS

Glue and nail the side pieces (those with three cutouts) over the edges of the end pieces. Hold the four sides square in clamps until dry.

PUTTING THE BOTTOM IN PLACE

Nail and glue a ledger around the inside of the four walls of the box, about 1 inch up from the bottom. Place the bottom panel inside the box on top of the ledger strips, and then drive screws up through the ledgers into the underside of the bottom panel.

HAT AND TOWEL RACKS

The typical colonial New Mexican home most likely had no use for bath and paper towel racks, and the most common hat and coat rack probably consisted of a wooden peg driven into the adobe wall. But again, by applying traditional New Mexican design features to everyday items, we can come up with uncommon accessories that add a touch of the Southwest to any room.

CUTTING LIST

Hat and Coat Rack
(38" x 6¼")

Part	Qty	T	W	L	Piece
A	1	¾"	5½"	34½"	Back
B	2	¾"	5½"	5½"	Ends
C	1	¾"	5½"	38"	Shelf
D	1	¾"	1¾"	38"	Shelf Front
E	5	¾"		3"	Dowel

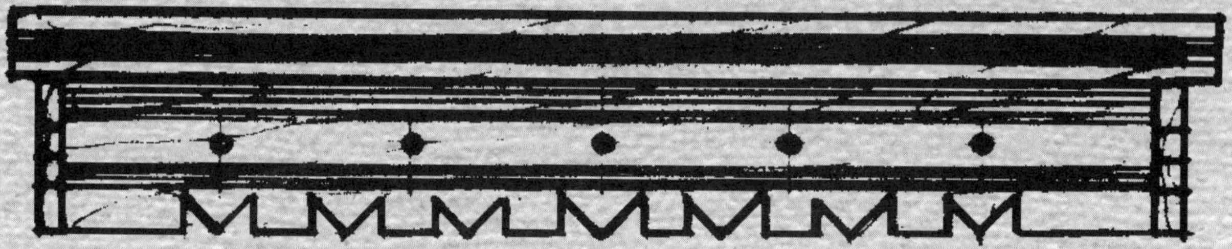

Hat and Coat Rack

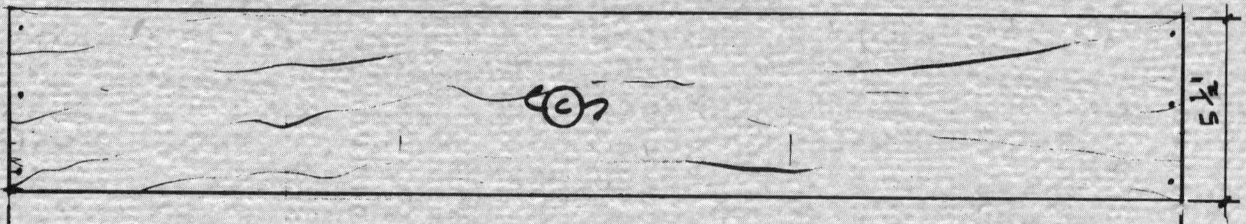

Shelf

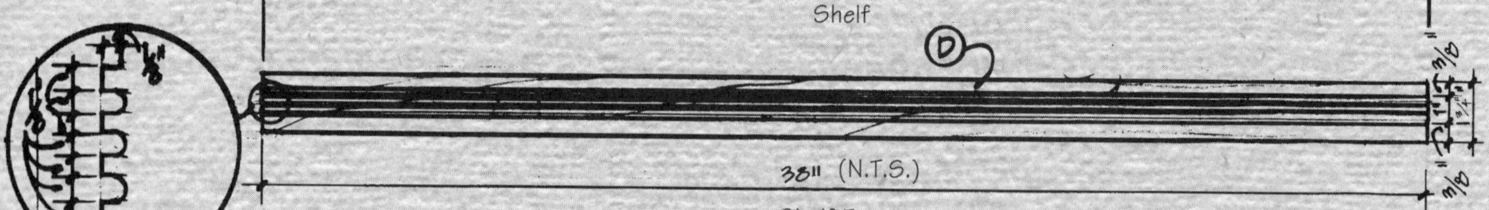

Shelf Front

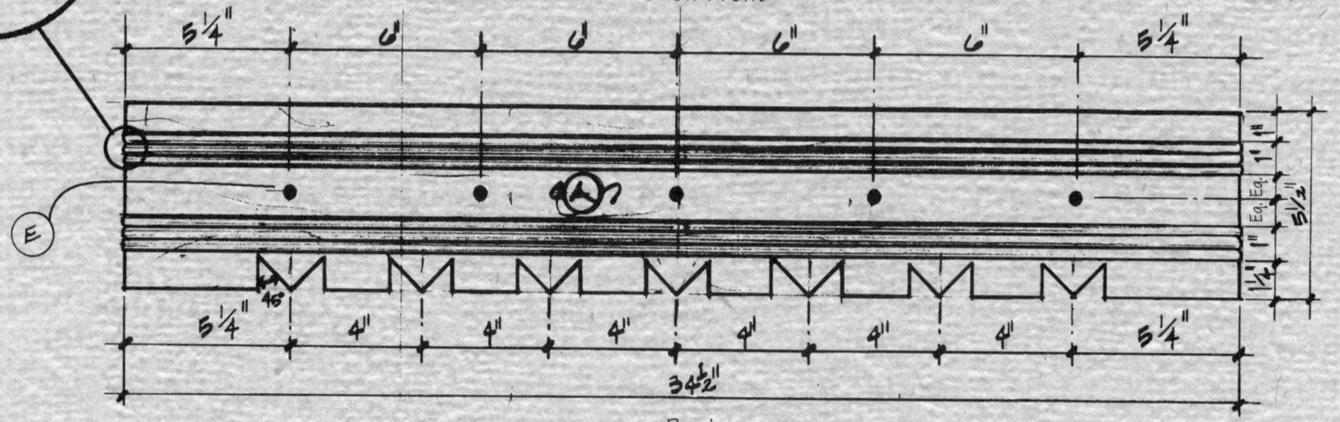

Back

HAT AND COAT RACK

Design

This hat and coat rack (see the illustration on page 40), with a shelf above for gloves and mittens, is loosely based on a nineteenth-century *repisa*, or small shelf, that is on loan to the Museum of New Mexico. A rack of this type typically hung outside the home under the portal and served as a coat closet. The original is 46 inches long and features seven hand-carved pegs. Feel free to make yours as long or short as you like, with as many pegs as you can comfortably use.

Creating the Embellishments

Run two three-bead grooves the length of the back piece, the first 1 inch down from the top and the second 1¼ inches up from the bottom. Run a similar three-bead groove the length of the center of the shelf front, as shown on page 40.

Lay out the "M" design along the bottom edge of the back and cut away the waste material with a band saw, back saw, or saber saw. You can cut any design you like into the end pieces. Drill ½-inch holes along the length of the back for your pegs, spaced about 6 inches apart.

Building the Rack

Glue and nail the end pieces to the ends of the back piece with a simple butt joint. Glue and nail the shelf to the top edge of the back and tops of the end pieces. Then nail the shelf front piece to the front of the shelf. Finally, carve a set of pegs with a ½-inch taper at one end and glue them into the holes.

Peg

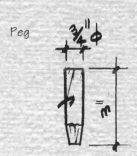

Ends

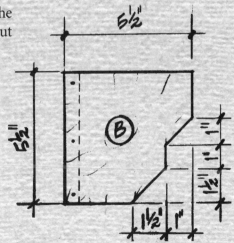

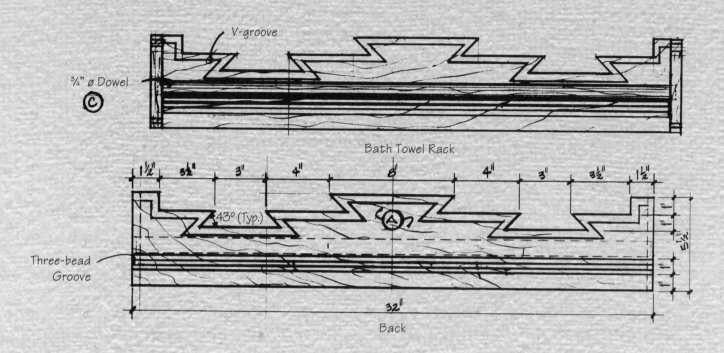

V-groove

¾" ø Dowel

Ⓒ

Bath Towel Rack

1½" 3½" 3" 4" 8" 4" 3" 3½" 1½"

43° (Typ.)

Ⓐ

Three-bead
Groove

5½"

32"

Back

CUTTING LIST

Bath Towel Rack
(32" x 5½")

Part	Qty	T	W	L	Piece
A	1	¾"	5½"	32"	Back
B	2	¾"	5½"	4"	Ends
C	1	¾"	n/a	to fit	Towel Bar

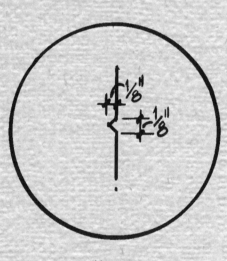

⅛"

⅛"

V-groove

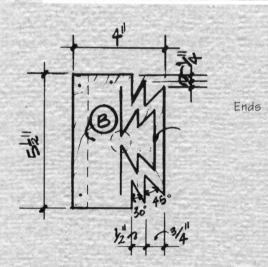

4"

Ⓑ

5½"

30° 45°

½" 3¼"

Ends

BATH TOWEL RACK

Design

This is a fixed-bar bath towel rack that will give a touch of the Southwest to any bathroom (see the illustration on page 42). The design is adapted from a bench that dates from the early years of the twentieth century. The bench was built in the then-popular Mission style, with the same New Mexican motif along the top of the back rail that I have incorporated into the back of this rack.

Creating the Back Piece

Run a three-bead groove the length of the back piece, begin-ning about 1-inch up from the bottom edge. Lay out the pattern along the top edge and cut it with a band saw or saber saw. Then carve a v-groove parallel to the cutout pattern, about ½ inch in from the top edge (see the illus-tration on page 42).

Creating the End Pieces

Draw two lines to connect the diagonally opposite sets of cor-ners, so the lines intersect in the middle of the piece. Drill a ⅜-inch-deep hole with a ¼-inch Forstner bit at the center point of the inside face of each end piece.

Cut a ¾-inch by ¼-inch rabbet in the back inside edge of the end pieces. Cut both end pieces with a pattern similar to that used on the back piece. Carve the outside face of the end piece with the same v-groove gouge as used above.

Assembling the Rack

Clamp the two ends to the back piece and measure the re-quired length of your towel rod. Cut the rod to length, tuck it into the shallow holes in the end pieces, then glue and nail the end pieces to the back piece.

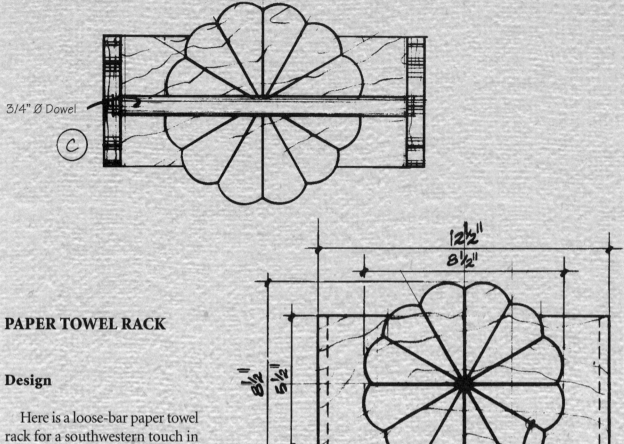

3/4" Ø Dowel

C

12½"

8½"

8½"

5½"

A

V-groove

Back

PAPER TOWEL RACK

Design

Here is a loose-bar paper towel rack for a southwestern touch in the kitchen (see the illustration above). Its design is a typical twelve-part rosette in the back, with eight-part rosettes carved into the ends.

Creating the Rosette Patterns

To create the rosette pattern on the back of the rack, draw diagonal lines across the piece to connect its corners, and scribe a circle from their intersection at the center tangent to the size of rosette you want to carve.

Draw horizontal and vertical lines through the center point to cut the circle into quadrants. With a compass set to the radius of the original circle, swing arcs in both directions from where the vertical and horizontal lines intersect the circumference of the circle to further divide the circle into twelve equal parts.

To draw an eight-part rosette, again draw diagonals across the end pieces, which in this case are square. Draw a circle tangent with the outside edge of the end pieces. Then draw horizontal and vertical lines through the center of the circle.

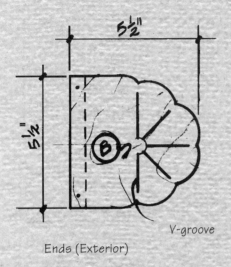

5½"

5½"

V-groove

Ends (Exterior)

¾" x ¼" Rabbet for Back Panel

¾"W. x ¼"D. Slot

Ends (Interior)

Making the End Pieces

Cut a ¾-inch by ¼-inch rabbet on the back inside ends of the end pieces. With a ¾-inch straight bit in the router set to a depth of about ³⁄₁₆ inch, cut a slot from the center point on the inside face of the end pieces up along the back center of the first petal of the rosette.

Cut the profile of the rosettes with a band saw, saber saw, or jig saw. Round over the cut edges with a ¼-inch-square chisel. Always work with the grain to prevent tear-out. Finally, carve the radii of each rosette with a v-gouge.

Assembling the Rack

Nail and glue the end pieces to the back piece, cut the towel bar to fit, and slide it into place.

CUTTING LIST

Paper Towel Rack
(12½" x 8½")

Part	Qty	T	W	L	Piece
A	1	¾"	8½"	12½"	Back
B	2	¾"	5½"	5½"	Ends
C	1	¾"	n/a	to fit	Towel Bar

REPISAS

Chances are, if a modest New Mexico home one hundred years ago had any decorative piece at all, it was a *repisa*, or small shelf, hanging on the wall. There the household may have displayed a crucifix, a *bulto* (a painted image of a saint), or a *santo* (a carved image of a saint). *Repisas* came in any number of designs and sizes and making them gave their creators the chance to embellish their work with imaginative carving, cutouts, and painting.

Most *repisas* had one long (up to 42 inches) shelf, with a decorative piece running the length of the front to stop objects from falling off. Though uncommon, multi-shelf *repisas* were not unknown. Two examples of two-shelf *repisas* are on display in the Museum of New Mexico, and they have located one example of a three-tier model.

All three of the following *repisas* are built the same way.

OVAL-END REPISA

Design

This design (see the illustration on page 47) was found in a book distributed to New Mexican vocational schools when Works Progress Administration woodworking programs were active during the 1930s.

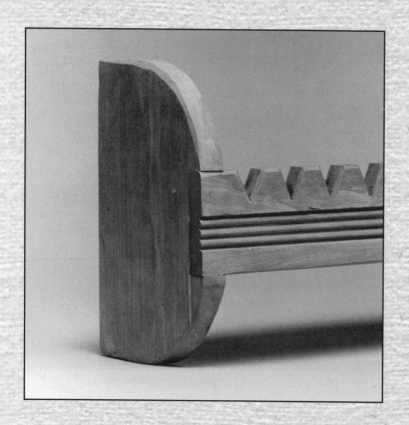

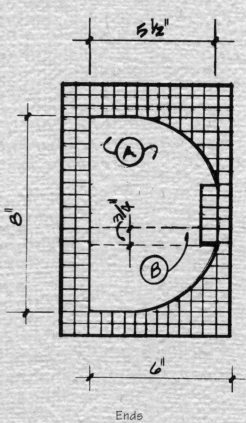

Ends

CUTTING LIST

Oval-end Repisa
(18" x 5½" x 8")

Part	Qty	T	W	L	Piece
A	2	¾"	5½"	8"	Ends
B	1	¾"	4¾"	17¼"	Shelf
C	1	¾"	2½"	18"	Shelf Front

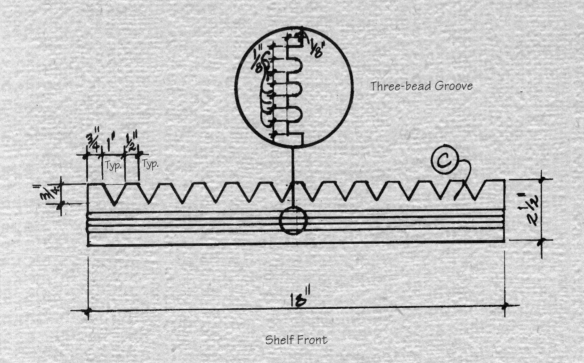

Three-bead Groove

Shelf Front

TWO-SHELF REPISA

Design

This design (see the illustration on page 49) was adapted from a nineteenth-century *repisa* which featured three vertical carved splats, or ornamental bars, running between the two shelves.

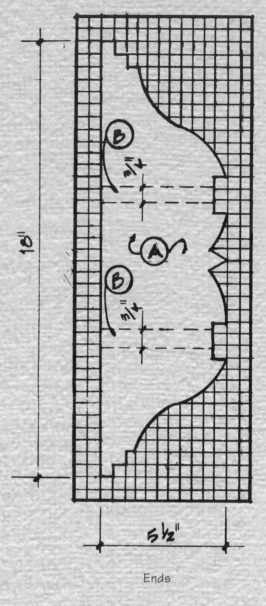

Ends

CUTTING LIST

Two-shelf Repisa
(24" x 5½" x 18")

Part	Qty	T	W	L	Piece
A	2	¾"	5½"	18"	Ends
B	2	¾"	4¾"	23¼"	Shelf
C	2	¾"	2½"	24"	Shelf Front

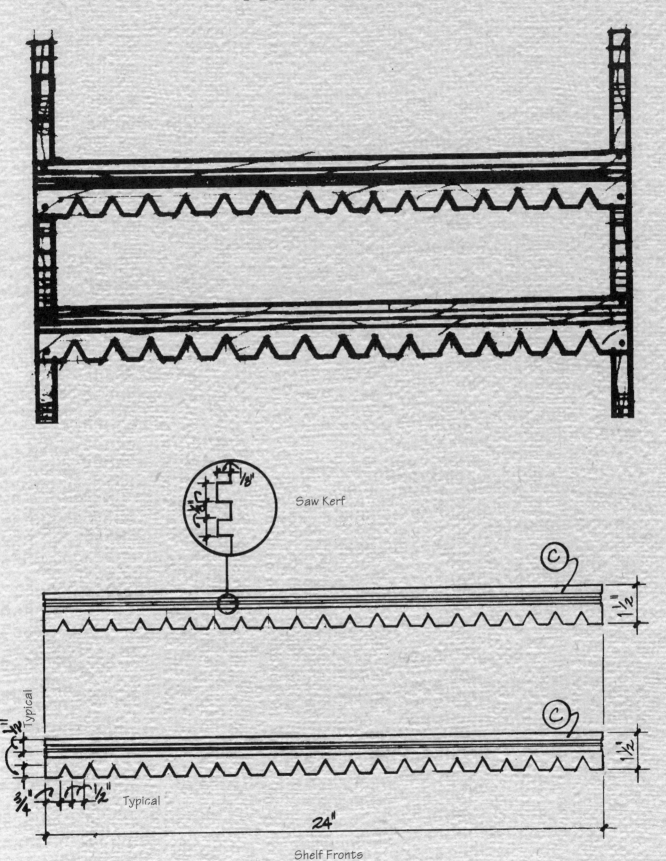

Saw Kerf

Typical

Typical

Shelf Fronts

SCALLOP-FRONT REPISA

Design

This *repisa* (see the illustration on page 51) is adapted from a nineteenth-century piece in the collection of the Museum of New Mexico. The original was 41 inches long and had the complicated front piece shown in the drawing. It was finished with gesso, and painted *santero*-style with scrolls and floral patterns. Make yours as long or short as you like, and decorate it to suit your own taste.

Making the Ends

Before you cut patterns into the end pieces, first cut a ⅜-inch-deep by ¾-inch-wide dado across the inside face of each (as shown above) to accept the shelf(ves). Next, when building the oval-end

and two-shelf *repisas*, cut two 1½-inch by ¾-inch notches in each end piece, centered over the shelf dado, to accept the shelf front piece. On the scallop-front *repisa*, the front piece overlaps the ends with a butt joint.

CUTTING THE END PATTERN

Draw a ½-inch grid on one piece of end stock, and lay out the pattern. Clamp or tack the two pieces together with the dados facing inward, and cut out the pattern on a band saw or with a saber saw.

Creating the Shelf Fronts

On the fronts that feature the sawtooth pattern, run a pair of shallow, ⅛-inch-deep kerfs the length of each shelf front piece, centered vertically between

top and bottom. (You may use the three-bead cutter, if you prefer.) Next, lay out the sawtooth or scallop pattern along the edge of each shelf front, and cut it out using a band saw or saber saw.

Assembling the Shelf

Glue and nail the shelf(ves) into the end piece dados. Then glue and nail the shelf front piece into place.

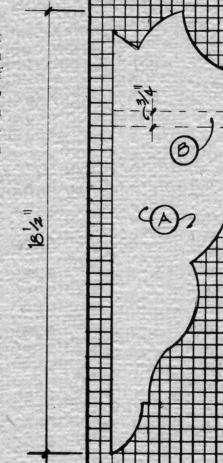

Ends

CUTTING LIST

Scallop-front Repisa
(24" x 5½" x 18½")

Part	Qty	T	W	L	Piece
A	2	¾"	5½"	18½"	Ends
B	2	¾"	5 ½"	23¼"	Shelves
C	2	¾"	2"	24"	Shelf Front

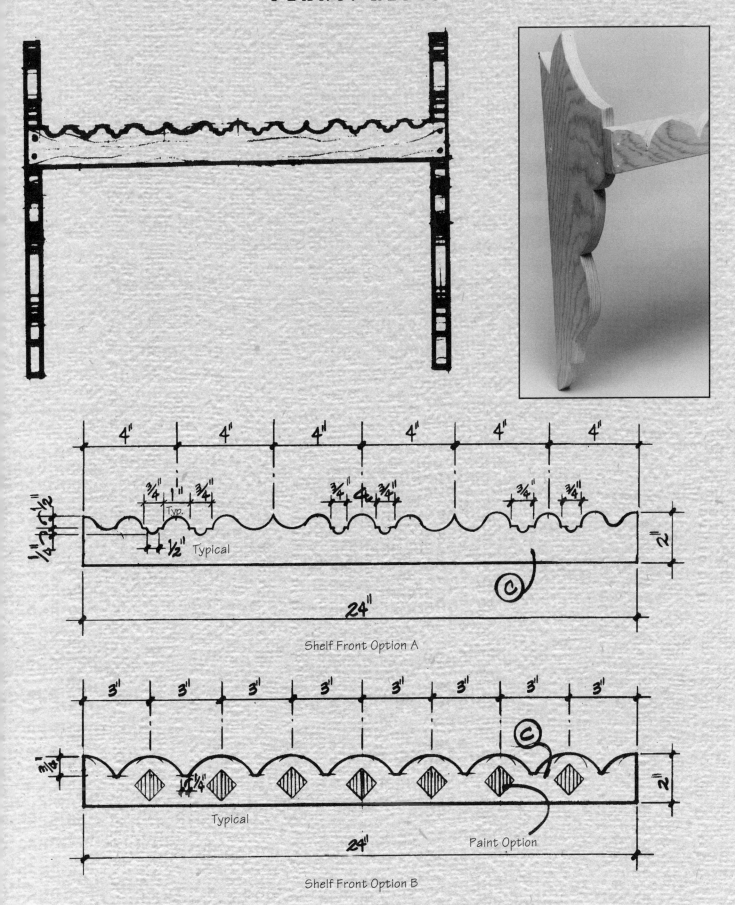

Shelf Front Option A

Shelf Front Option B

51

BLANKET CHESTS

PEÑASCO CHEST, EIGHT-SQUARE CHEST, CROSS CHEST, AND STEP CHEST

Chests are the form of colonial New Mexican furniture which best survived the rigors of time. They were commonly used to store household goods and food and are generally divided into three categories: board chests; frame chests; and false-frame chests, which combine elements of the first two. Those designed as shipping trunks had no legs. In the home, a pair of simple stands kept each box elevated and prevented its rotting on the dirt floors.

Design

The advent of nails allowed carpenters to build simple boxes which they embellished with fancy cutouts and moldings. Each of these four chests is built in the same manner—the only difference is their ornamentation. The overall design was adapted from nineteenth-century originals built in the false-frame style.

CUTTING LIST

Blanket Chests
(37½" x 18½" x 25¼")

Part	Qty	T	W	L	Piece
A	2	¾"	18"	34"	Front & Back
B	2	¾"	18"	14½"	Sides
C	1	¾"	14½"	32½"	Bottom
D	1	5/4"	18½"	37½"	Top
E1	4	¾"	3"	24"	Front & Back Leg Pieces
E2	4	¾"	1¾"	24"	Side Leg Pieces
F	4	¾"	3"	29½"	Front & Back Trim
G	4	¾"	3"	12½"	End Trim
H	These pieces will vary according to the particular design; cut them to fit, according to the drawings.				Detail Pieces
I	1	¾"	1"	to fit	Ledger Material

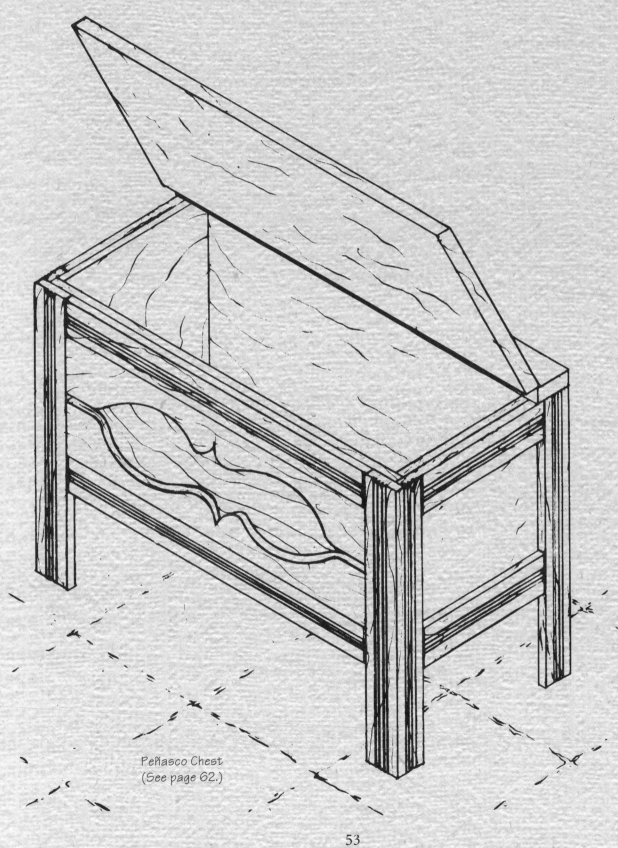

Peñasco Chest
(See page 62.)

Building the Box

To form the front, back, side, and bottom panels of the chest, edge-glue together the appropriate number of one-by boards. (You can also use plywood, but it's not very authentic.) Glue and nail the front panel onto the front edges of the two side panels. Then nail the back piece onto the back edges of the two side panels.

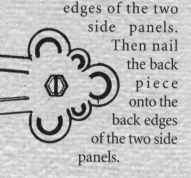

Strap Hinge

PUTTING THE BOTTOM IN PLACE

Glue and screw a ¾-inch ledger around the inside of the four walls of the box, flush with the bottom edges. Place the bottom panel inside the box top and fit it into place so it rests on the ledger strips. Then drive 1¼-inch sheetrock screws up through the bottom of the ledger strips into the underside of the bottom panel to hold it in place.

Making the Trim Strips and Legs

Run a three-bead groove the length of the trim pieces and the four front leg pieces, centered in the middle of the boards. Then run the same bead the length of each side leg piece along one edge, so that when they are nailed to the

Side View

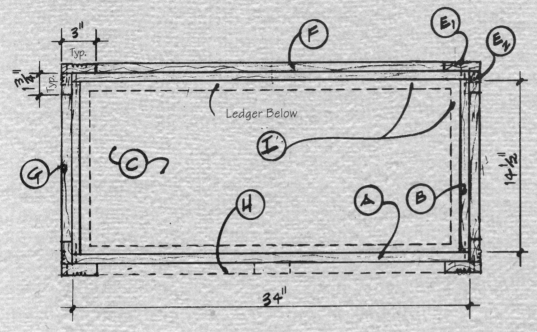

Plan View

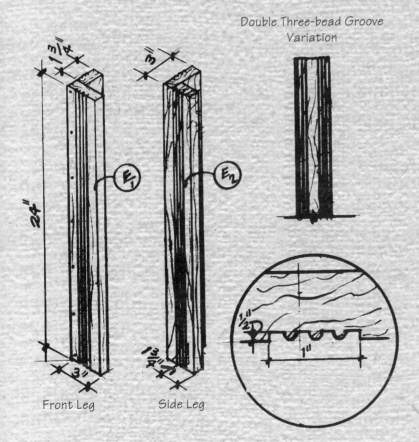

Double Three-bead Groove
Variation

Front Leg

Side Leg

Three-bead Groove

front pieces the side grooves appear to be in the center. Then, while your box is clamped and setting, edge-glue and nail (using a simple butt joint) the four front leg pieces onto the four side leg pieces to create four legs (see the illustration on this page).

Attaching the Legs and Trim

Glue and nail the four legs to the outside corners of the box, so their tops are flush with the top of the box. Then nail the horizontal trim pieces to the top and bottom edges of the front, back, and side panels of the box.

At this point, glue and nail one of the four decorative patterns onto the front surface of the chest.

Note: The exact dimensions of the various decorative pieces have been left off the cutting list. Sim-

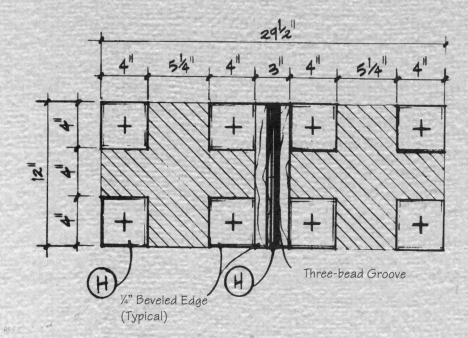

29½"

4" 5¼" 4" 3" 4" 5¼" 4"

4"
4"
12"
4"
4"

Three-bead Groove

H

H

¼" Beveled Edge
(Typical)

Eight-square Trim Pattern

ply follow any of the drawings, and cut the particular decorative pieces to fit. The eight-square and step designs (shown here and on page 60) each have an additional piece of front vertical trim that separates the front panel into two parts. The little crosses on the corner blocks of the eight-square design are carved with a v-gouge. The ends of the trim pattern pieces on the cross design (shown on page 58) are cut at 45-degree angles to form the cross.

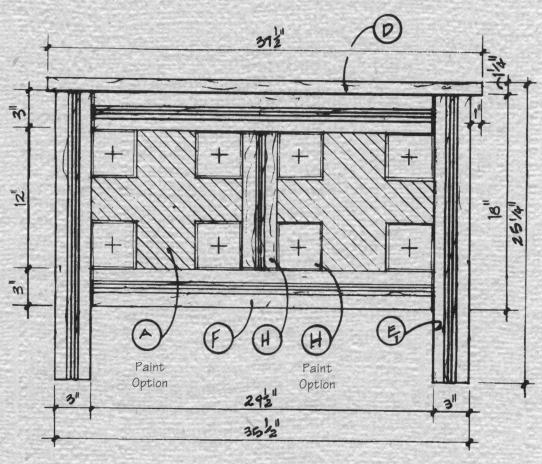

31½"   D

2¼"

3"

1"

12"

18"
25¼"

3"

A   F   H   H   E

Paint
Option   Paint
Option

3"   29½"   3"

35½"

Front View

Fabricating the Chest Top

Rip a 3-inch strip off the back edge of the top. Align it with the back of the box, countersink holes for screws, and fasten the strip to the back and side edges. Plug the countersunk holes with dowels and sand smooth.

Attach the rest of the top to this strip with a pair of large strap hinges. Although you may not be able to find a pair of hinges as nice as those shown in the drawing on page 54, see Hardware in the Overview section for a source for hand-wrought hinges imported from Mexico.

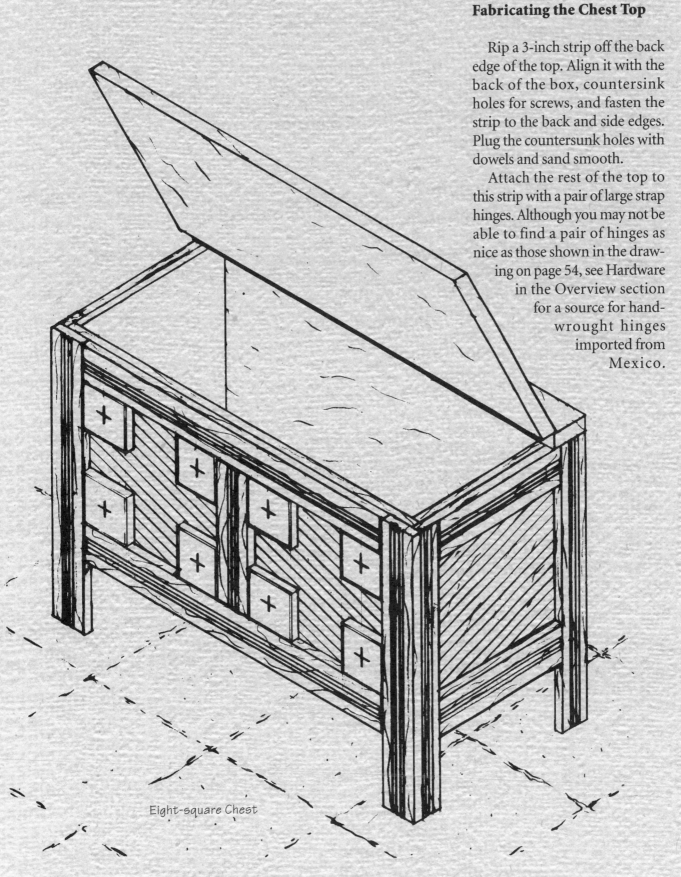

Eight-square Chest

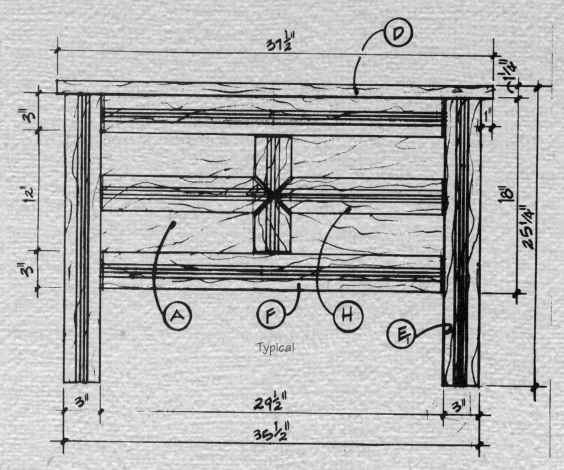

Front View

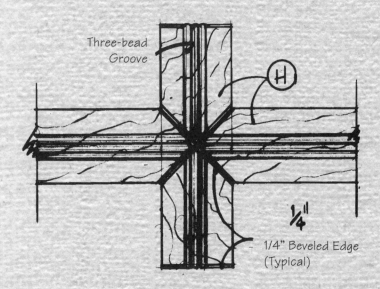

Three-bead Groove

1/4" Beveled Edge (Typical)

Cross Trim Pattern

Finishing the Chest

Finish the chest with a combination of stain and paint to suit your taste. I generally stain the legs, trim pieces, and top with a light pine stain. I then go back and paint the base of the box and the trim in contrasting colors.

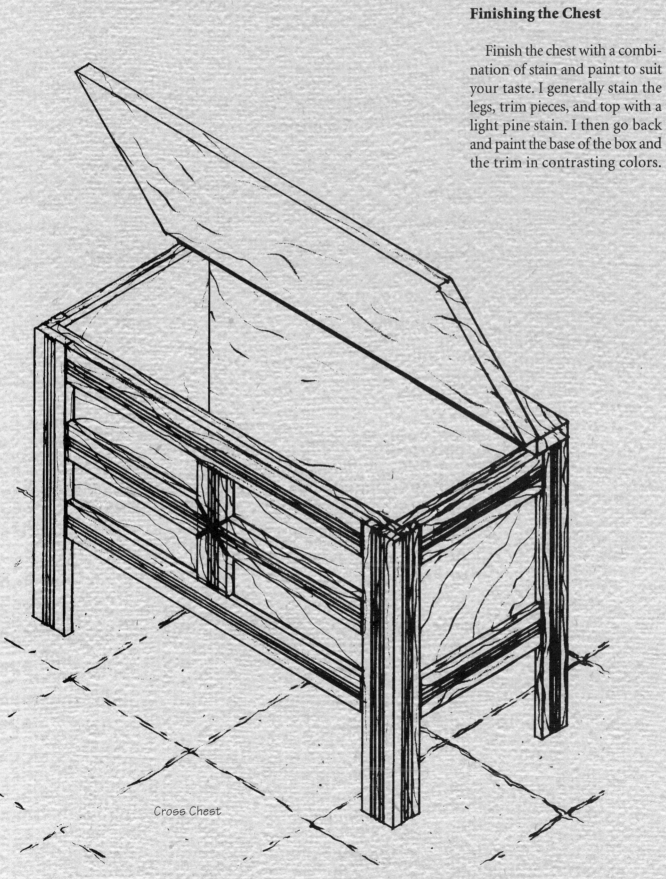

Cross Chest

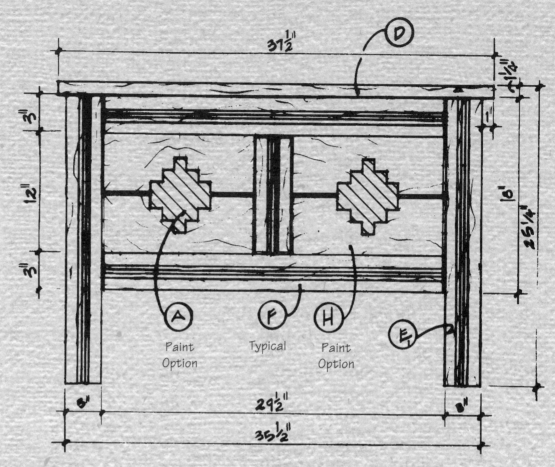

Front View

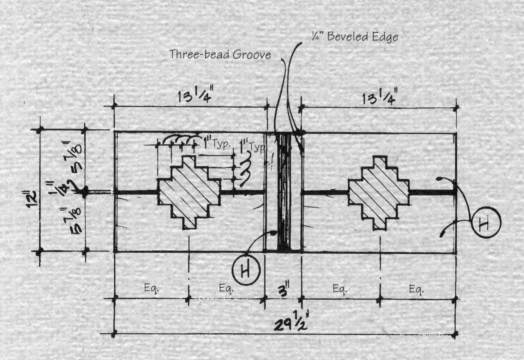

Step Trim Pattern

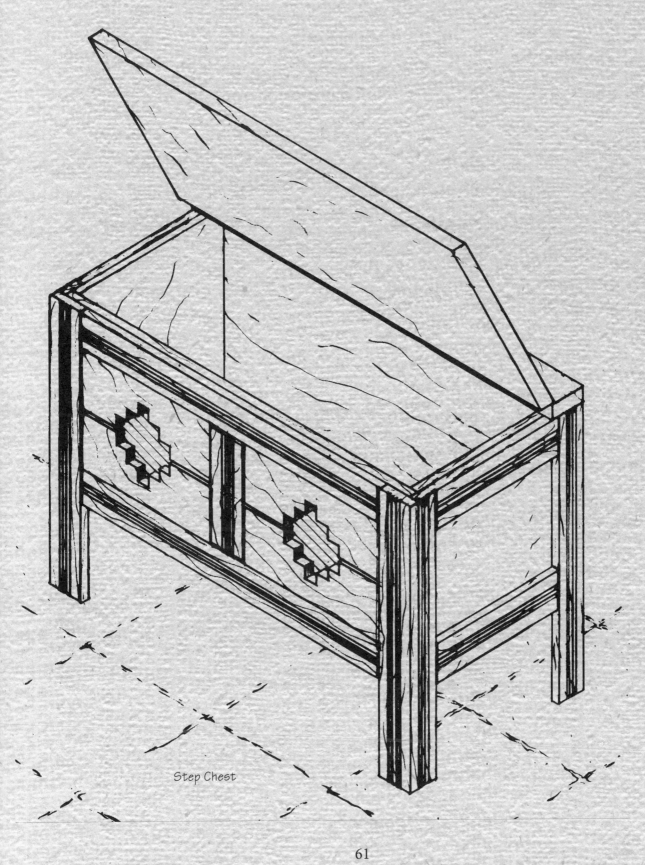

Step Chest

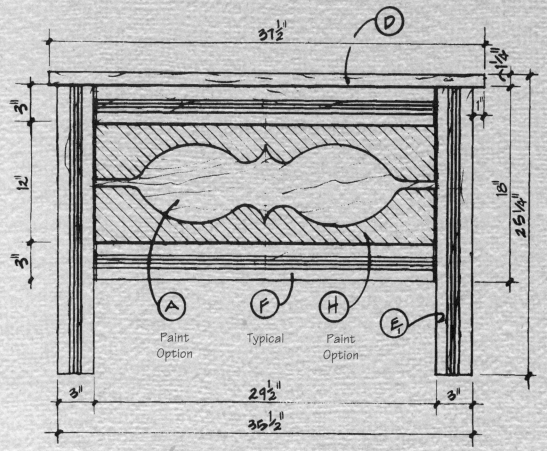

37½"　Ⓓ　2½"

3"

12"

3"

1"

18"

25¼"

Ⓐ　Ⓕ　Ⓗ　Ⓔ₁

Paint　Typical　Paint
Option　　　　Option

3"　29½"　3"

35½"

Peñasco Chest: Front View

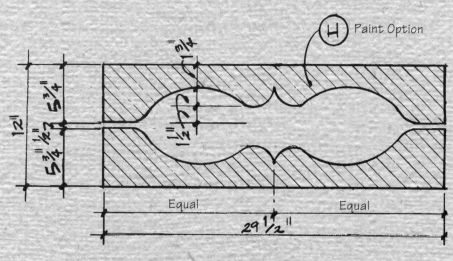

Ⓗ Paint Option

12"

5¾"

½"

5¾"

¾"

⅞"

1½"

Equal　Equal

29½"

Peñasco Trim Pattern

FOOTSTOOLS

Aside from the *bancos*, or benches, which were built into the adobe walls of many New Mexico homes, the *tarima*, or small stool, was the most common form of seating. *Tarimas* sat a little higher than footstools and looked like small tables. In fact, they were often used as serving tables upon which food was brought from the kitchen. Their low profiles allowed people to sit close to a fire for both warmth and light.

RECTANGULAR FOOTSTOOL, SQUARE FOOTSTOOL

Design

The two footstools offered here draw upon this tradition and can be considered *tarimas* with upholstered tops. They are built in the same manner, and fit together

much like a table, with the aprons mortised into the legs (or fastened with pegs) and the top screwed to the aprons. (For added strength, you might want to add stretchers, which connect the legs at points closer to the floor.)

These plans show two different apron patterns, but the dec-

CUTTING LIST

Rectangular Footstool
(23½" x 11½" x 17")

Part	Qty	T	W	L	Piece
A	4	2½"	2½"	15"	Legs
B	2	¾"	5½"	19¾"	Long Aprons
C	2	¾"	5½"	8"	Short Aprons
D	1	¾"	11½"	23½"	Top
E	2	¾	1"	to fit	Ledgers

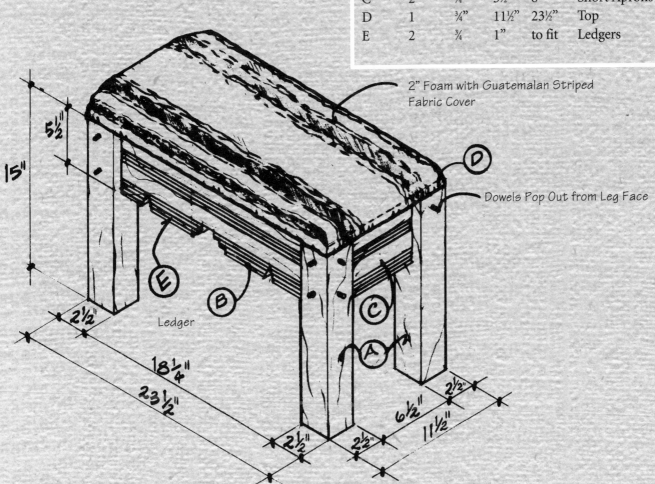

2" Foam with Guatemalan Striped Fabric Cover

Dowels Pop Out from Leg Face

Ledger

5½"

15"

2½"

18¼"

23½"

2½"

2½"

6½"

2½"

11½"

CUTTING LIST

Square Footstool
(14" x 14" x 14¾")

Part	Qty	T	W	L	Piece
A	4	2⅜"	2⅜"	11¾"	Legs
B	4	¾"	4½"	10¾"	Aprons
C	1	¾"	14"	14"	Top
D	2	¾"	1"	to fit	Ledgers

orative possibilities are endless (see pages 70–71). Feel free to experiment with your own ideas to develop unique designs.

Building the Leg and Apron Frame

DECORATING THE APRONS
   If you plan to use mortise-and-tenon joints on the aprons, cut the tenons first. Then, run a three-bead cutter twice down the length

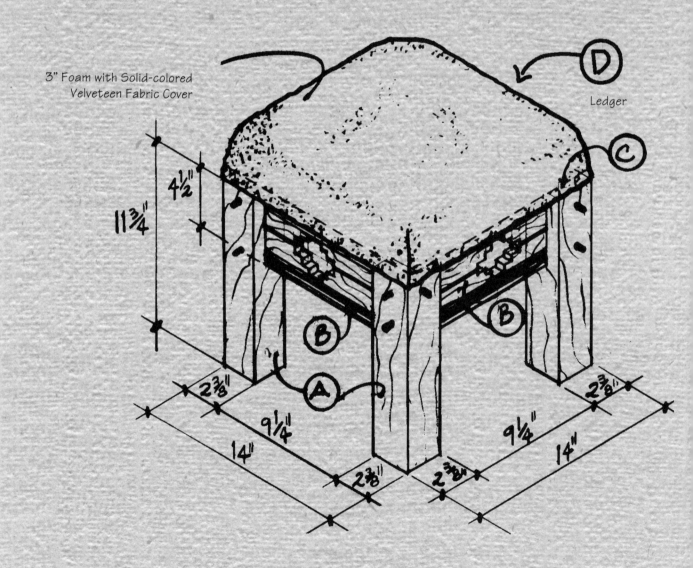

3" Foam with Solid-colored
Velveteen Fabric Cover

Ledger

of each apron piece, once about 1 inch down from the top edge and once about 1 inch up from the bottom edge.

CREATING THE CUTOUTS

To create the negative space pattern, begin by ripping each apron piece in half horizontally. Clamp all four pieces together, with the edges just ripped facing up. Lay out your pattern on the face, along the top edge of the stack. Remove the waste with a radial arm saw, saber saw, and/or back saw. When you remove the clamps and put each set of halves back together, you will see the negative space pattern you have created.

Other patterns, like the one on the rectangular stool shown on page 63, are cut into only one edge of the apron. To create them, clamp both apron pieces together and cut out your pattern as described above.

ASSEMBLING THE LEG AND APRON FRAME

Dry-assemble the legs and the aprons, then drill two ⁵⁄₁₆-inch holes into the legs *through* the apron tenons. When the legs and aprons have been glued and clamped, add pegs for strength. You can leave them standing a little proud for a handcrafted look.

Upholstering the Top

First make sure your top is as wide as the outside dimension of the leg and apron assembly. Next, cut out a 2- or 3-inch-thick piece of foam on the band saw, the same size as the top, and place the top piece and foam together. Now you can attach your fabric, which should be about 6 inches longer and wider than the top. Staple the side flaps to the top first, adjusting the tension of the fabric to keep it smooth. Pull the four corners toward the bottom center of the top and staple them. Finally, staple the end flaps in place, making sure to create a sharp crease at each corner.

Attaching the Top

Screw ledger strips to the inside faces of the two longer apron pieces, flush with the top edge. Place the top upside down, and lay the leg and apron assembly onto the underside of the top. Center it, then screw through the bottoms of the ledger strips into the underside of the top.

TABLES

Traditional New Mexican tables were usually heavy affairs featuring through mortise-and-tenon overlapping joints held in place by wooden pegs and strong stretchers to secure the legs. The aprons were generally fairly deep and lavishly embellished with chip and bullet carving and cutouts.

HALL TABLE, END TABLE, MIRROR TABLE, AND COFFEE TABLE

Design

The tables featured here are far easier to build than traditional pieces, but incorporate the same southwestern design elements. Included in the plans are designs for four different apron patterns (see the illustrations on pages 70–71) and dimensions for four tables, but you can play with them to suit your needs. Make the coffee table shown on page 74 smaller, add a piece of foam and fabric covering, and you have a footstool. The hall table shown on page 67 can sit just as easily behind a couch; make it wider, and it's a kitchen table. Build it wider and longer for a dining table. The combinations

CUTTING LIST						
Hall Table (48" x 12" x 29")						
Part	Qty	T	W	L	Piece	
A	4	2½"	2½"	27¾"	Legs	
B	2	¾"	5½"	43½"	Long Aprons	
C	2	¾"	5½"	7½"	Short Aprons	
D	1	1¼"	12"	48"	Top	
E	4	1¼"	2½"	6"	Corner Blocks	

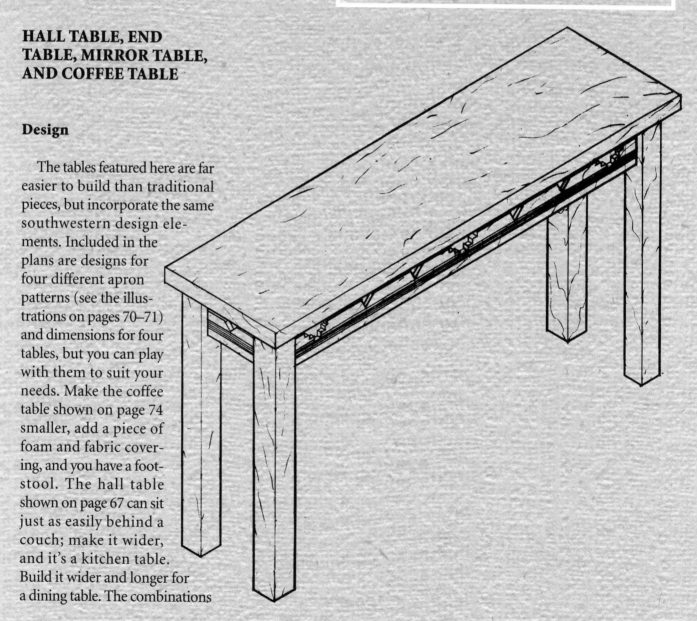

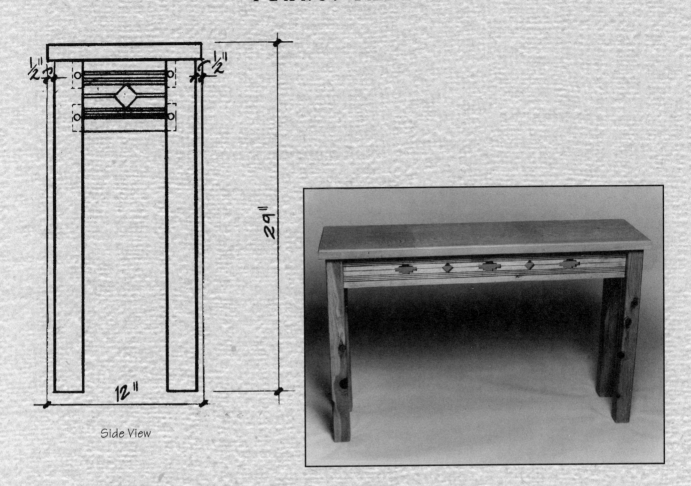

1/2"

29"

12"

Side View

1/2"

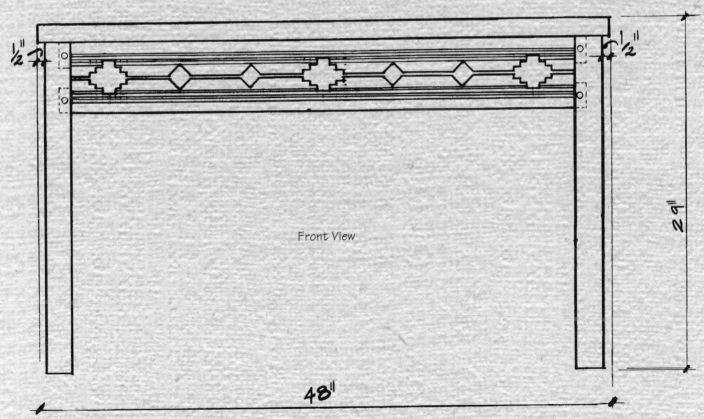

1/2"

1/2"

29"

Front View

48"

are endless. Use the basic construction details over and over, vary the apron designs to suit your taste, and you'll have the perfect table for any specific need.

Building the Leg and Apron Frame

The dimensions shown give apron depths of 5½ inches (conveniently cut from 1-inch by 6-inch material). For a kitchen or dining room table, however, comfortable seating requires at least 6 inches between the bottom of the apron and the top of the chair seat. In that case, reduce your apron accordingly.

Decide what kind of leg-to-apron joint you plan to use before making your aprons. If you are going to use a mortise-and-tenon joint (as shown on pages 20–22), cut the apron tenons before cutting any detail into the aprons. This will help eliminate chipping the three-bead grooves where they meet the tenons.

DECORATING THE APRONS

Begin your apron design by twice running a three-bead cutter the length of each apron piece, once about 1 inch down from the top edge and once about 1 inch up from the bottom edge (see the illustrations on pages 70–71).

CREATING THE CUTOUTS

For patterns utilizing the concept of negative space, rip each apron piece in half horizontally. Clamp all four pieces together, with the edges just ripped facing up. Lay out your pattern on the face and along the top edge of the stack, and mark the right-hand side for depth. Remove the waste with a radial arm saw, saber saw, and/or back saw (see the illustration below). When you remove the clamps and put each set of halves back together, you will see the negative space pattern you have created.

The other patterns are cut into only one edge of the apron. To create them, clamp both apron pieces together and cut out your pattern as described above.

DECORATING THE LEGS

If you wish, you can relieve the blank look of the legs by running a three-bead cutter down the length of the outside faces, a single bead down two sides of the outside corner, or a chamfer or bullnose down three (or even all four) corners of each leg.

ASSEMBLING THE LEG AND APRON FRAME

Dry assemble the legs and aprons, then drill two 5/16-inch holes into the legs *through* the apron tenons. When the legs and aprons have been glued and clamped, add pegs for strength. You can leave them standing a little proud for a handcrafted look.

Making The Top

Generally, a table top should hang about 1 inch over the outside edges of the legs. However, when there is a cutout along the top edge of the apron, a full inch will sometimes hide the pattern. Consequently, the drawings

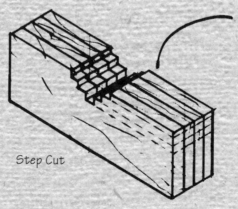

Cut Four Apron Patterns at One Time

Step Cut

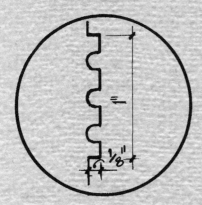

Three-bead Groove

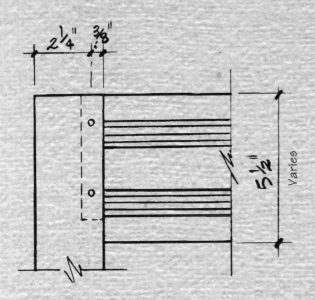

Leg and Apron Views

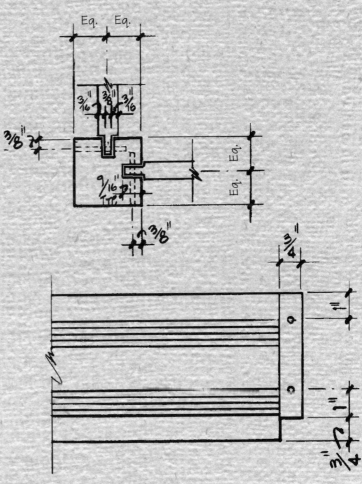

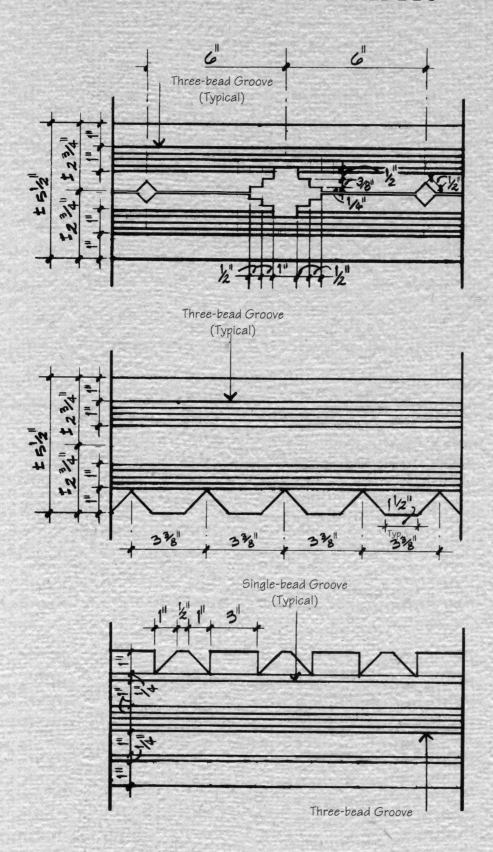

Apron Variations

Three-bead Groove
(Typical)

Three-bead Groove
(Typical)

Single-bead Groove
(Typical)

Three-bead Groove

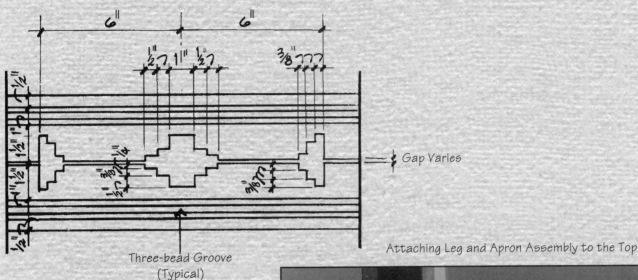

Three-bead Groove
(Typical)

Gap Varies

Attaching Leg and Apron Assembly to the Top

shown here call for a ½-inch overhang. Experiment and do what looks best to you.

The cutting lists for these tables call for tops made from ¾-inch material. The following describes another way to make the top, using ¾-inch material to make it appear double-thick.

Begin in the usual fashion by edge-gluing a series of boards to achieve a top of the desired width. Trim the top to the desired width, except cut the length 3 inches short. Dowel and glue a 1½-inch-wide breadboard strip to each end.

Cut four 4-inch-wide pieces of ¾-inch material to the lengths of the sides and ends, and glue and clamp them to the underside edges of the top. Round the corners of the top, and knock off the square edges with a bullnose in your router. The result will be an interesting combination of end grains at the corners.

Fastening the Top to the Leg and Apron Assembly

Cut four 6-inch-long corner blocks and put 45-degree angles on each end to make them roughly triangular, as shown above. Drill countersink holes into the blocks, and screw them to the inside faces of the aprons, flush with the top edges.

Lay the leg and apron assembly on the underside of the top, align it, and screw through the corner blocks (use oversize holes to allow for some expansion) into the underside of the top.

CUTTING LIST

End Table
(16" x 16" x 24")

Part	Qty	T	W	L	Piece
A	4	2½"	2½"	22¾"	Legs
B	4	¾"	5½"	11½"	Aprons
C	1	1¼"	16"	16"	Top
D	4	1¼"	2½"	6"	Corner Blocks

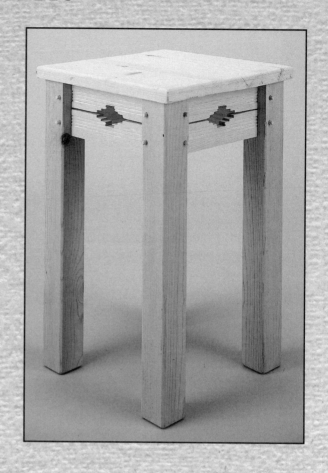

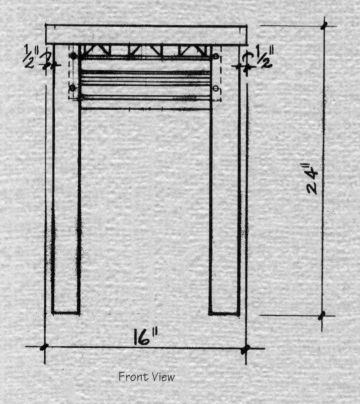

Front View

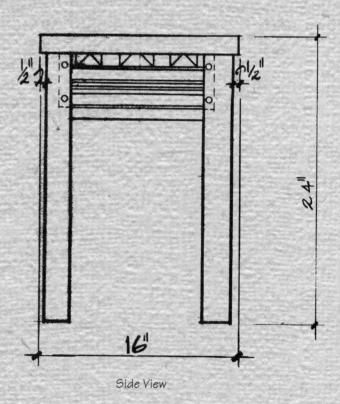

Side View

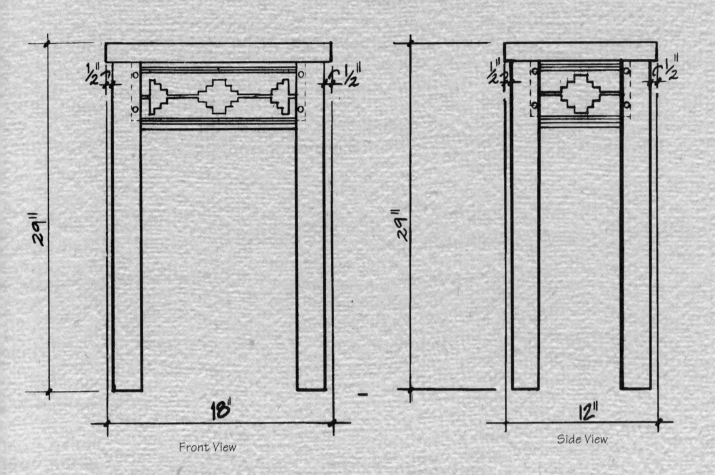

Front View

Side View

CUTTING LIST

Mirror Table
(18" x 12" x 29")

Part	Qty	T	W	L	Piece
A	4	2½"	2½"	27¾"	Legs
B	2	¾"	5½"	13½"	Long Aprons
C	2	¾"	5½"	7½"	Short Aprons
D	1	1¼"	12"	18"	Top
E	4	1¼"	2½"	6"	Corner Blocks

CUTTING LIST

Coffee Table
(36" x 18" x 18")

Part	Qty	T	W	L	Piece
A	4	2½"	2½"	16¾"	Legs
B	2	¾"	5½"	31½"	Long Aprons
C	2	¾"	5½"	13½"	Short Aprons
D	1	1¼"	18"	36"	Top
E	4	1¼"	2½"	6"	Corner Blocks

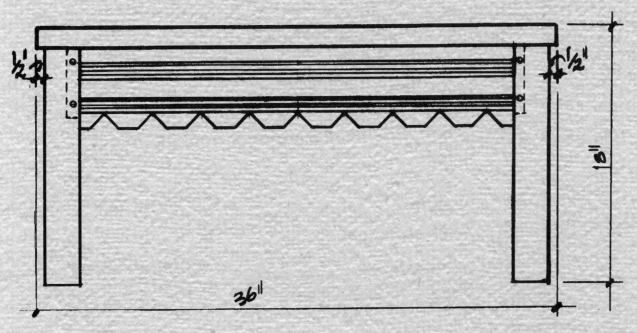

Front View

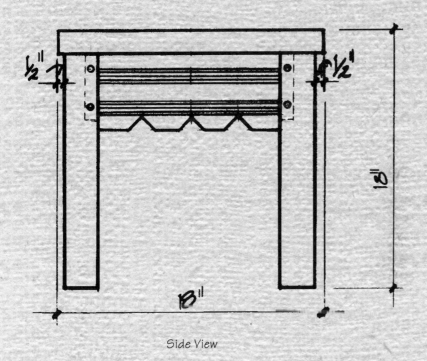

Side View

BEDS

The bed in the traditional New Mexico home was a narrow slab affair, little more than a long, low table. Although beds these days are more elaborate, making them to suit today's tastes (and mattress sizes) can be very satisfying. They're fairly easy to build, and the headboards are like massive canvases upon which to practice and display your carving. Since you spend at least thirty percent of your life in a bed, it might as well be a nice one.

Design

Every bed consists of a headboard, a footboard, four posts, and two side rails with ledgers to hold up the slats upon which the mattress sits. The only hard and fast rule when making a bed is that it be big enough to accept the mattress for which it has been designed. Beyond that, it is a blank slate upon which you can explore your own creative and artistic energy. When finished, you will have a family heirloom that should last several generations.

Standard Steps

There are certain steps common to the construction of every bed. Let's run through those before we look at the specifics associated with building the three plans featured in this book.

Fabricating the Pieces

The beds offered here call for legs about 2½ inches to 2¾ inches square. If you can't find 1¾-inch stock, rip eight pieces of two-by material and laminate them

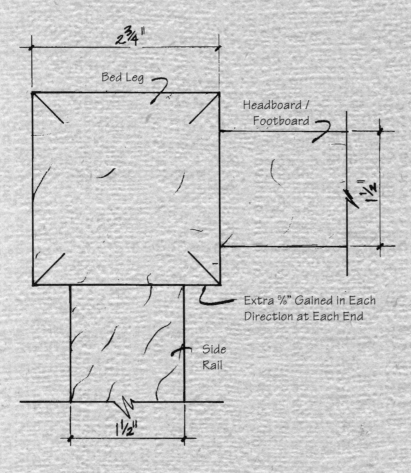

Post and Headboard Detail: Plan View

together into four pairs. Strips of wax paper laid between laminations will prevent one pair from accidentally becoming glued to another while all four are laid up in clamps at one time.

If the headboard and footboard are to be large solid pieces, edge-glue panels together to achieve the desired size. I like to also use ⅜-inch dowel pins for extra strength. Make sure to cut your headboard at least 4 inches wider than the width of the mattress. This gives you plenty of material for tenons and for the bed to be a little wider than the mattress. Keep in mind that set-

ting a 1½-inch-thick headboard (and footboard) and side rails into the center of a 2¾-inch post already adds 1¼ inches to the inside width (and length) of the bed (see drawing on page 76 to calculate additional lengths and widths). This allows blankets and quilts to be tucked in comfortably. Determine for yourself if you want any additional space.

Building the Bed

CREATING THE JOINTS

Once the inside width of the headboard and footboard are

determined, draw vertical lines to mark the outside edges. Clamp a straight edge along each line, and, using the straight cutter in the router, remove ⅜ inch of waste from the fronts and backs of the headboard and footboard, creating a ¾-inch-thick by 1½-inch long tenon. Then cut a ½-inch shoulder on the top and bottom outside corners of the headboard and footboard.

With the same ¾-inch straight cutter in the router, cut a ¾-inch-thick by 1½-inch-deep mortise down the inside face of each post to match the headboard and footboard tenons.

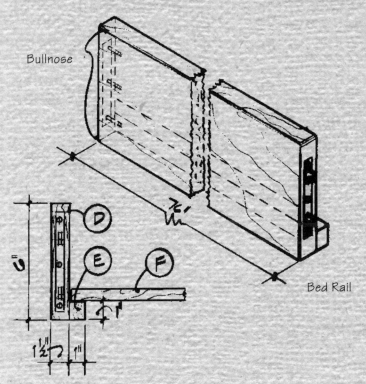

Bullnose

Bed Rail, Ledger, and Mattress Planks

Bed Rail

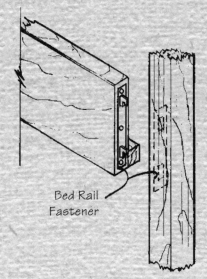

Bed Rail Fastener

ADDING THE SIDE RAILS

The side rails on a bed that will not use a box spring should sit about 10 inches off the floor. If you plan to use a box spring, lower the rails to about 7 inches high. Use a bullnose router to smooth the top inside and outside edges and the bottom outside edge of the rails. Keep the bottom inside edges square.

You can fasten the rails to the headboard and footboard with either through or blind mortise-and-tenon joints and hold them in place with large dowel pins for easy disassembly. Another way is to use 6-inch iron bed rail fasteners (see Hardware in the Overview section for a supply source). Properly installed, they snap together and yield a snug joint. When cutting slots for the rail fasteners into the posts and rails with a ⅝-inch straight cut router bit, remember that for a tight fit it is essential that the fasteners be absolutely flush with the surface.

LAYING IN THE BOTTOM PLANKS

The last step is to glue and screw a 1-inch ledger along the bottom inside edge of the side rail, and lay in ¼-inch planks on top, on which to rest the mattress or box spring.

SINGLE BED

Design

This design features the traditional step-and-diamond motif featured on the Indian trade blankets of the old West (see the illustrations on pages 79 and 80). The planks in the headboard and footboard are set with ¼-inch spaces between them, and the top edges of the top planks and the bottom edges of the bottom planks are embellished with a three-bead cutter.

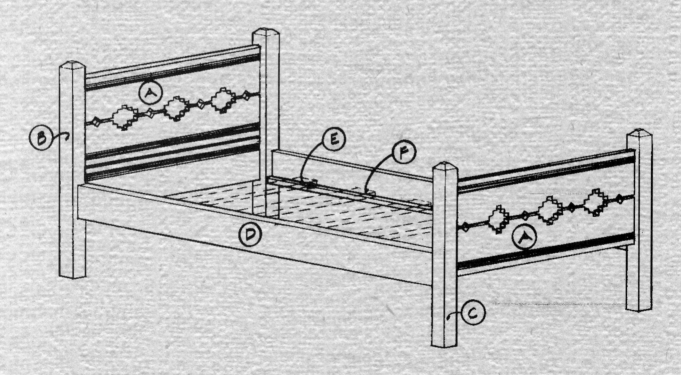

CUTTING LIST

Single Bed
(43½" x 80½")

Part	Qty	T	W	L	Piece
A	5	¾"	6"	41"	Headboard and Footboard Planks
B	2	2¾"	2¾"	32"	Headboard Legs
C	2	2¾"	2¾"	26¼"	Footboard Legs
D	2	⁵⁄₄"	6"	75"	Side Rails
E	2	1"	1"	75"	Ledgers
F	6	¾"	12"	40"	Slats

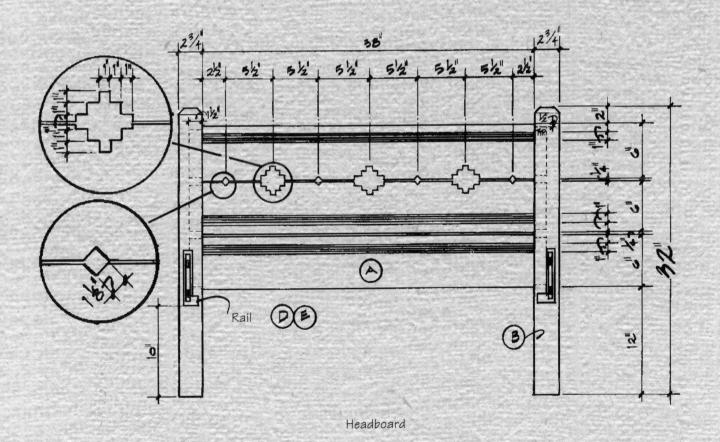

Headboard

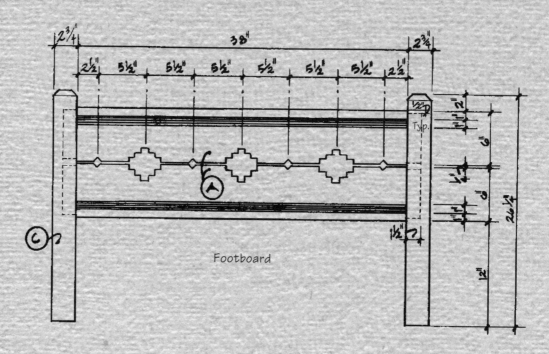

Footboard

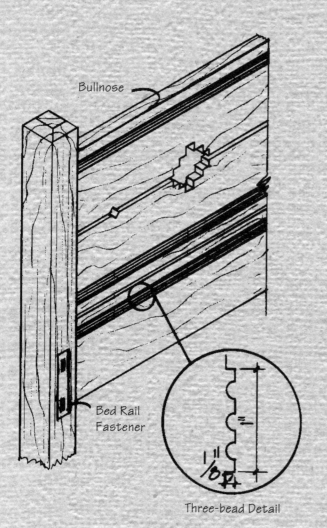

Bullnose

Bed Rail Fastener

Three-bead Detail

Building the Headboard and Footboard

Begin by cutting the headboard and footboard planks to length. Make sure, whatever the size of the bed you are making, to add sufficient material to allow for a 1-inch tenon on each side.

The first step is to cut a ⅜-inch-thick by 1-inch-long tenon on the ends of each plank. Do this before using the three-bead cutter to prevent the beads from chipping out when the tenons are cut across them.

Next, run the three-bead cutter down the length of each plank (on both sides in the case of the footboard) beginning about 1 inch in from one edge.

Cut a ½-inch shoulder on the top outside corners of the two top planks and a similar shoulder on the bottom outside corners of the two bottom planks.

CREATING THE NEGATIVE SPACE PATTERN

Clamp together the pairs of planks to be used for the negative space pattern. Make sure the sides with the three-bead design are facing in. Lay out your step-and-diamond design on the plank facing you, and along the top edges of the planks. Mark the right-hand edge for depth.

Begin by finding the center point in the length of the planks, then work your design to the outside edges in the symmetrical pattern of your choice. Remove the square material with the dado cutters in your radial arm saw (or with a saber saw), and cut the diamonds with a back saw. Remember that you are cutting out one-half of the finished design in all of the planks at once. When the planks are put back together edge-to-edge, the full design appears.

Take a block plane and carve a slight bevel along the length of the edges of each plank. Then carve a slight bevel on all the hard edges of the cutout design and where the edges of the tenons will meet the mortises in the legs.

Making the Legs

Cut a ⅜-inch-wide by 1-inch-deep mortise down the inside face of the legs, starting 2½ inches from the top of each leg. Cut each mortise long enough to accept the combined tenons on each set of headboard and footboard planks. Remember to allow for a ¼-inch gap between planks.

Bevel and sand the tops of all four legs so they are smooth and rounded. Glue the plank tenons into the leg mortises, using ¼-inch pieces of Masonite or other material as spacers between the planks.

Installing the Fasteners, Fabricating and Installing the Side Rails and Slats

Follow the instructions in the double bed design to fashion the rails, ledgers, and slats, and attach the bed rail fasteners (see the illustrations on page 77).

DOUBLE BED

Design

In this particular design, the headboard and footboard have the same shape. The legs are the heights of the headboard and footboard, respectively, with the footboard and its legs 10 inches shorter than the headboard and its legs.

Building the Headboard, Footboard, and Legs

Start by gluing together a series of ¾-inch planks, 57 inches long, to widths of 34 inches for the headboard and 24 inches for the footboard. Three inches of width will be used for a 1½-inch tenon on each side. As the planks

dry in their clamps, mill out or glue up four 2¾-inch square legs, 42 inches long for the headboard and 32 inches long for the footboard.

Cut a three-bead or other decorative line (if you like) around each of the four legs, starting about 3 inches down from the top. Bevel and sand the tops of the legs so they are rounded and smooth.

LAYING OUT THE SUNBURST DESIGN

Clean up any dried glue, and lay out the same sunburst design on both the headboard and footboard (see the illustrations on pages 83 and 84).

On both the headboard and footboard, measure down from the top and strike three horizontal lines, 2 inches apart. Draw a perpendicular line down the cen-

ter of each piece. Measure out from the center line along the top of each piece in 9-inch increments (or any dimension that comfortably splits the piece into six equal parts) and draw vertical lines down from those points. Connect the points where the vertical and horizontal lines intersect to the point at bottom center of each piece. Now you have a fan with six panels.

Follow the directions under Sunburst in Design Details of the Overview section to scribe the descending arcs. The result is a six-arc fan that drops 6 inches from the center to the edges. Cut a three-bead or other groove along the bottom edge of the headboard and footboard.

Scribe a smaller semicircle on both the headboard and footboard at the bottom of the center above the line of decorative

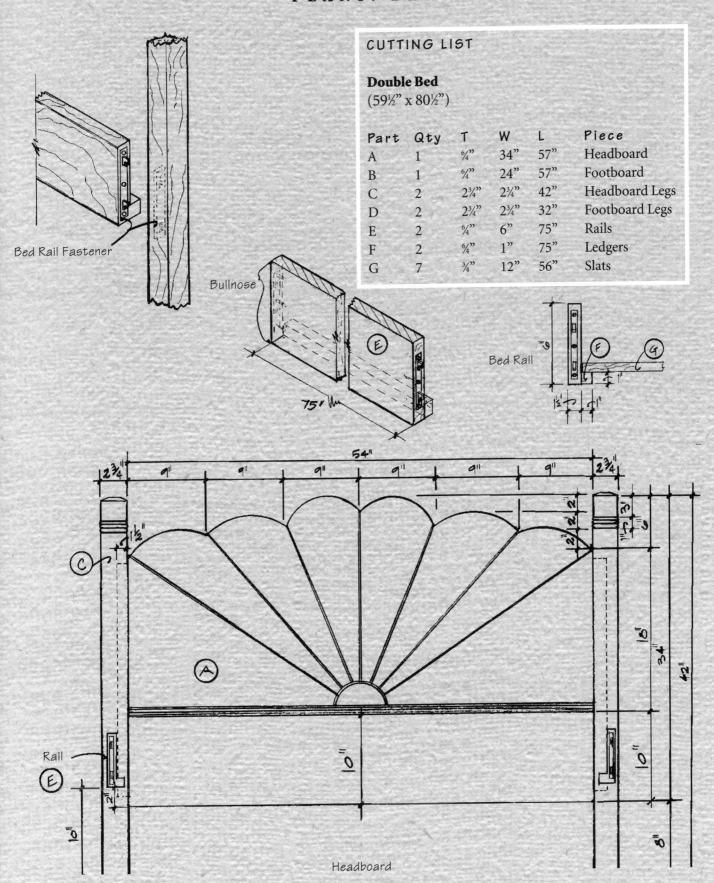

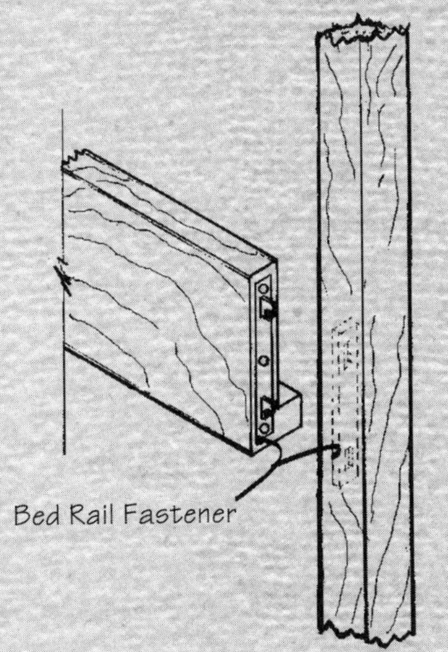
Bed Rail Fastener

CUTTING LIST

Double Bed
(59½" x 80½")

Part	Qty	T	W	L	Piece
A	1	5/4"	34"	57"	Headboard
B	1	5/4"	24"	57"	Footboard
C	2	2¾"	2¾"	42"	Headboard Legs
D	2	2¾"	2¾"	32"	Footboard Legs
E	2	5/4"	6"	75"	Rails
F	2	5/4"	1"	75"	Ledgers
G	7	¾"	12"	56"	Slats

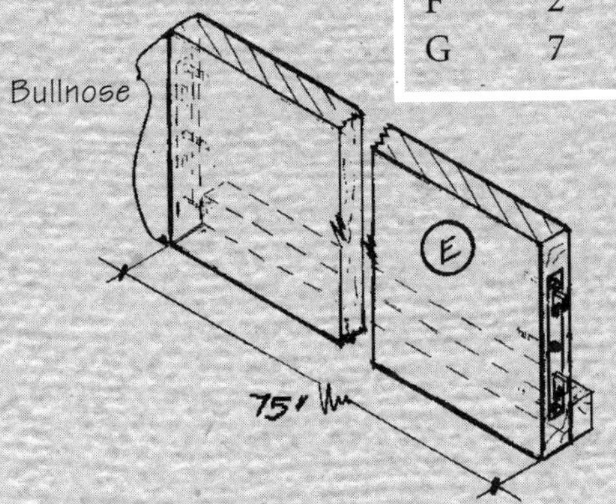
Bullnose
E
75"

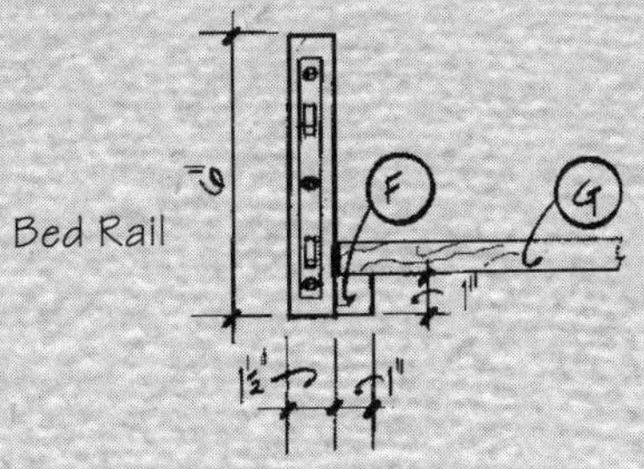
Bed Rail
6"
F
G
1"
1½"
1"

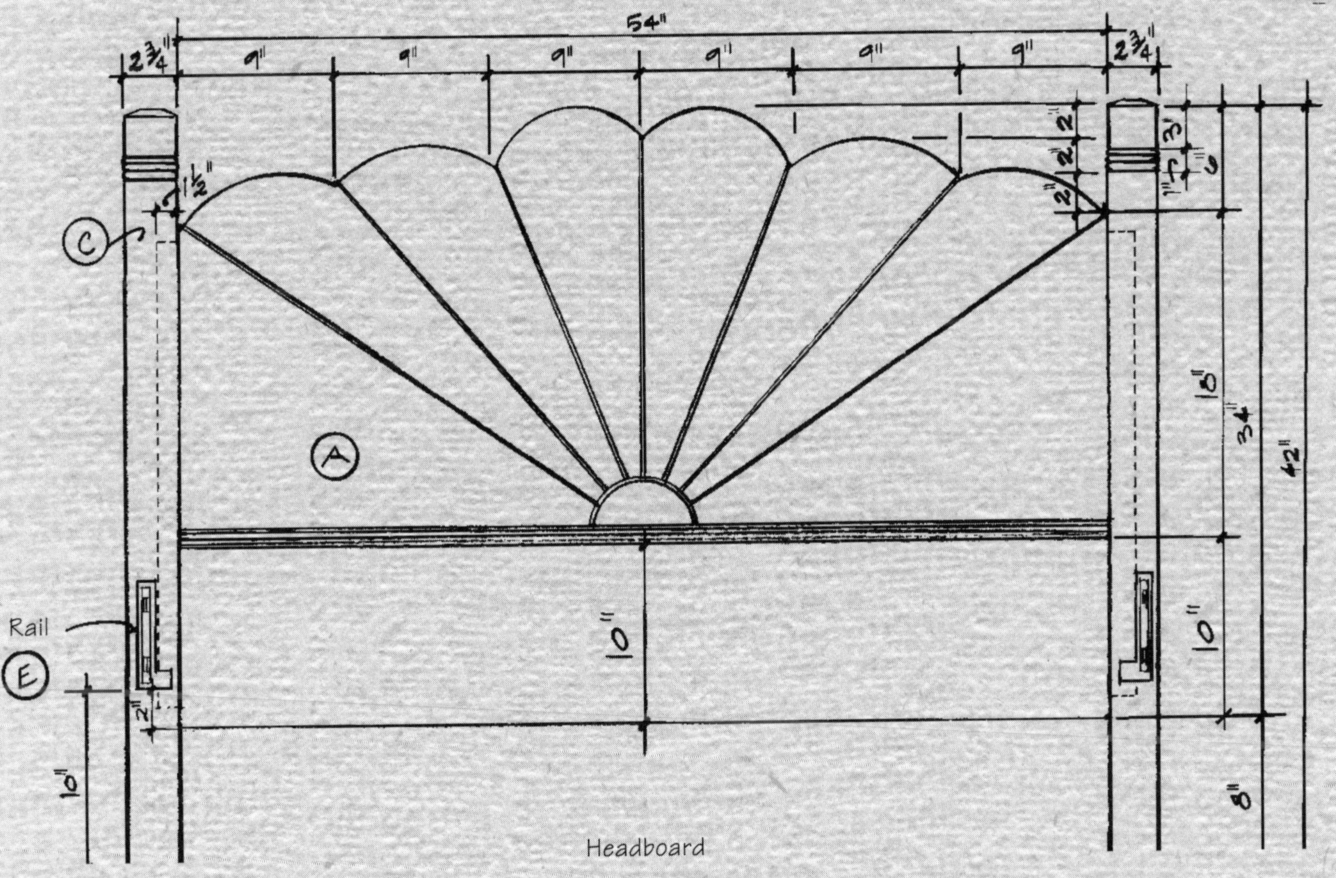
54"
2¾"
9"
9"
9"
9"
9"
9"
2¾"
C
A
Rail
E
10"
18"
34"
42"
8"
Headboard

grooves, so the seven fan lines all come to a stop at the semicircle.

Cut the scalloped line along the top edges of the headboard and footboard with a saber saw, and sand away the teeth marks. Then knock off the sharp edges with a bullnose cutter in the router.

Clamp a fence parallel to the center line and follow the line with a v-groove cutter in your router. Cut a similar groove along each of the other six fan lines and the semicircle at the bottom.

NOTE: The sunburst pattern need not show on the back of the headboard. It is nice, however, to have it on both sides of the footboard.

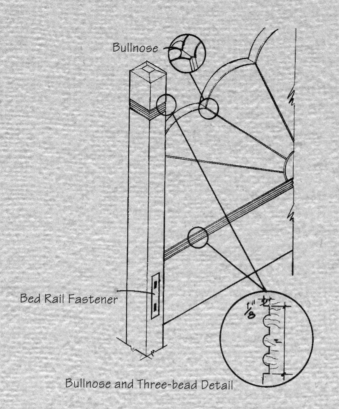

Bullnose

Bed Rail Fastener

Bullnose and Three-bead Detail

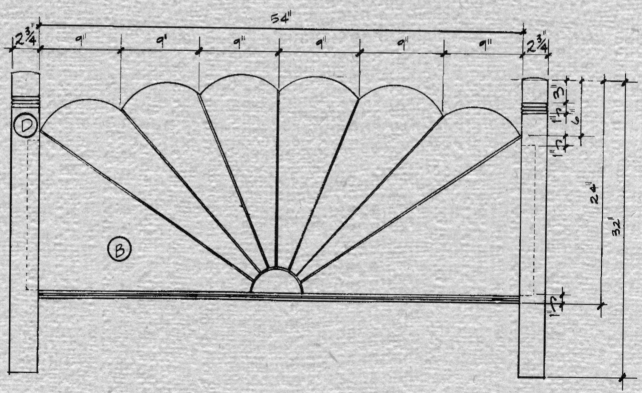

Footboard

Attaching the Legs to the Headboard and Footboard

Cut a long tenon on the ends of the headboard and footboard (as described above), and cut a ½-inch shoulder at the top and bottom of both sides of both pieces. Cut a mortise the length of the tenon into the inside face of the legs. Note: If you bevel the sharp edges on the headboard and footboard where they meet the mortise-and-tenon joints, you will get nice reveals that hide any ragged edges left showing when the headboard and footboard are glued to the legs.

Installing the Bed Rail Fasteners

Scribe the outline of the bed rail fastener vertically into the center of each leg, with the bottom edge of the fastener positioned approximately 10 inches up from the bottom of the leg (see the illustration on page 83). Attach a fence to your router and cut a slot with a straight cutter just deep enough for the bed rail

fastener to fit flush with the leg. Cut matching slots on the ends of the rails to accept the mating pieces of the bed rail fasteners. Use good long wood screws to hold the bed rail fasteners to the rails and legs.

Fabricating the Side Rails

Round over the top inside and outside and bottom outside edges of the side rails with the bullnose cutter, leaving the bottom inside edge square (see the illustration on page 83). Glue and screw a 1-inch-square ledger along the inside bottom edge of each side rail to support the mattress slats (see the illustration on page 83).

Cutting and Installing the Slats

With the side rails clipped into the legs, measure the distance between the rails, and cut enough 1-inch by 12-inch slats to form a platform for the mattress. Insert the slats so they rest on top of the ledgers.

SINGLE DAY BED

Design

This day bed is designed to hold a single bed mattress and to double as a couch. It can be modified, both in length and depth, to fit any size mattress or cushion. Its back rail features the traditional southwestern sunburst design, and the rails and vertical slats are embellished with three-bead grooves.

The two ends, the back, and the front rail are each made as a separate unit. The ends are joined to the back and front with through mortise-and-tenon joints held in place with ½-inch dowel pegs. Simply pull out six pegs and the bed folds into four flat pieces for convenient storage or transport.

Building the Back and Sides

EMBELLISHING THE SLATS AND RAILS

Run a three-bead cutter the length of the center of both sides of the vertical slats for the back and the sides. Run the same three-bead cutter the length of the center of the bottom side rails and the front rail.

ASSEMBLING THE BACK AND SIDES

Lay the back bottom rail on top of the back top rail, face to face, and mark the positions of the thirteen back verticals (see the illustration on page 87).

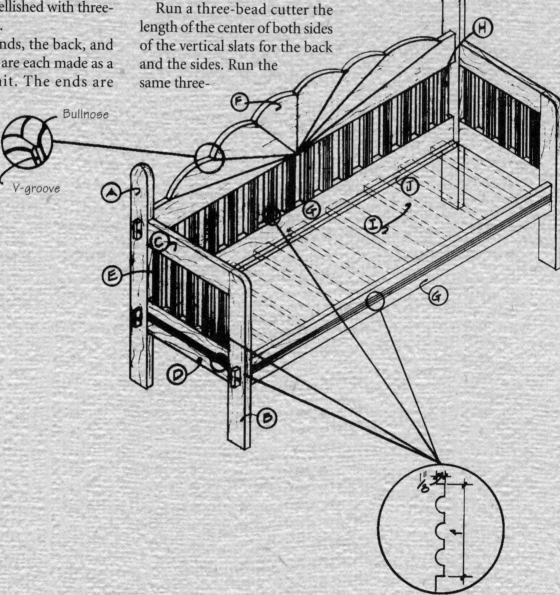

Bullnose

V-groove

Three-bead Detail

CUTTING LIST

Single Day Bed
(86" x 36")

Part	Qty	T	W	L	Piece
A	2	2"	6"	36"	Back Legs
B	2	2"	6"	30"	Front Legs
C	2	2"	6"	39"	Side Arms
D	2	2"	8"	39"	Bottom Rails (Sides)
E	10	2"	4"	7"	Vertical Slats (Sides)
F	1	2"	12"	86"	Top Rail (Back)
G	2	2"	8"	86"	Bottom Rails (Front & Back)
H	13	2"	4"	8¾"	Vertical Slats (Back)
I	7	1"	12"	39"	Bottom Slats
J	2	1"	1"	80"	Ledgers
K	1	½"		3'	Dowel
L	4	⅜"		3'	Dowel

(Dimensions reflect construction grade lumber.)

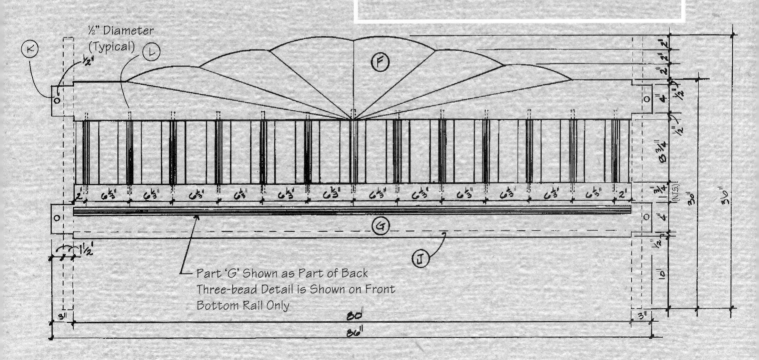

Part 'G' Shown as Part of Back
Three-bead Detail is Shown on Front
Bottom Rail Only

Back Piece

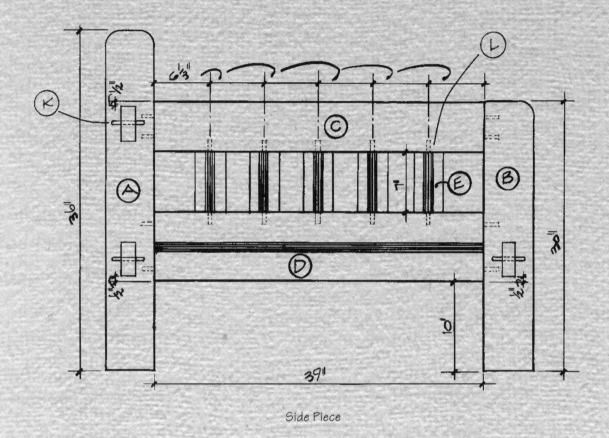

Side Piece

Using a Dowel-It jig, drill ⅜-inch holes for dowel pins. Do the same for the two arms, then glue and assemble the three units.

ROUNDING OFF THE ARMS

Using a gallon can or other circular shape, scribe an arc on the top corners of the legs (see the illustration above), and cut the shapes with a saber saw.

CREATING THE SUNBURST

Lay out a sunburst design on the back top rail as described in the instructions for the double bed design on page 82. Scribe the arcs with a flexible batten, and cut the scallops with a saber saw.

Sand out the teeth marks and round the sharp edge with a bullnose router cutter. Cut the fan lines with a v-groove router cutter.

Making the Mortise-and-Tenon Joints

Cut ½-inch shoulders on the ends of the top and bottom back rails and on both ends of the front rail, creating tenons that are 4 inches wide and 3 inches long. Cut matching through mortises into the legs.

Assembling the Bed

Assemble the piece by slipping the tenons through the mortises. Mark a spot for a ½-inch hole in the center of each protruding portion of tenon. Take the bed apart, drill the holes, and put it back together with six ½-inch dowel pins.

Glue and screw a 1-inch ledger to the inside bottom edge of the front and back bottom rails, and insert the horizontal slats to support the mattress.

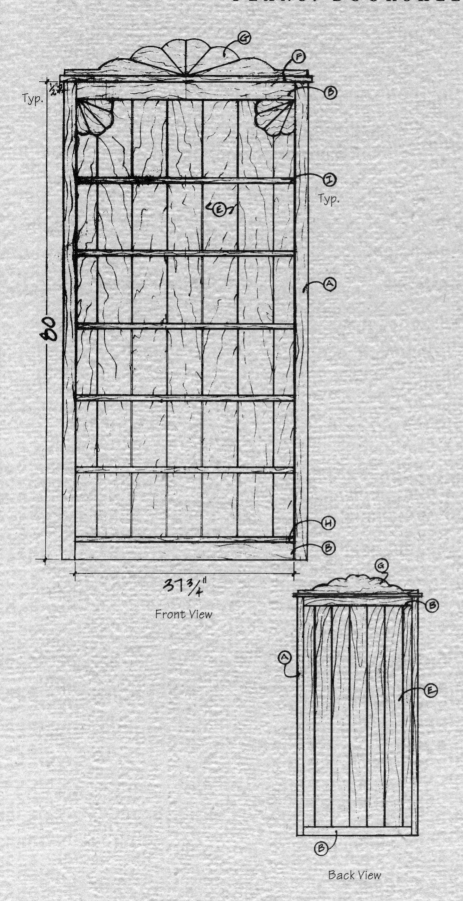

Front View

Back View

BOOKSHELF

Design

Most rooms can use an extra bookshelf, whether for books, stereo equipment, or collectibles, and a pair can attractively flank the sides of a doorway or fireplace. Build them deeper than drawn to accommodate bigger books.

This particular shelf has the traditional southwestern sunburst design on the top and in the corners, a pattern that can be repeated in the bottom rail if you like. The shelves are supported by pegs in holes spaced 2 inches apart, which allow the shelves to be adjusted to accommodate different size books.

Making the Legs and Rails

Cut a ½-inch-deep by ½-inch-wide dado down the length of each opposing face of the four legs and four side rails, to fit the side panels. Cut the same size dado down the length of each opposing face of the back legs and back top and bottom rails to accept the back panels (see the illustration on page 90).

Cut a ½-inch-wide by ¾-inch-deep mortise into the top and bottom of each leg to accept the four side rails and the four top and bottom rails (see the illustration on page 90).

Cut a ½-inch-wide by ¾-inch-long tenon on each end of the front and back top and bottom

89

rails and the top and bottom side rails.

Making the Side and Back Panels

Cut ½-inch-wide tenons around all four edges of the side panels, on the tops and bottoms of the back panels, and along the two outside side panels that will slip into the back of the back legs. Plane a bevel around the exposed perimeter of the side panels to suggest a raised panel look (see the illustration below).

CUTTING LIST

Bookshelf
(42¾" x 11" x 87¼")

Part	Qty	T	W	L	Piece
A	4	2"	2"	80"	Legs
B	4	2"	4"	39¼"	Front & Back Rails
C	4	2"	6½"	8"	Side Rails
D	2	¾"	7½"	73"	Side Panels
E	7	¾"	6"❖	73"	Back Panels(T&G)
F	1	5⁄4"	11"	42¾"	Top
G	1	5⁄4"	6"	42¾"	Top Sunburst
H	1	¾"	8"	to fit	Bottom
I	5	¾"	8"	to fit	Shelves
J	1	¼"		3'	Dowel

❖ Add ½" to outside edges of outside panels to allow for tenons.

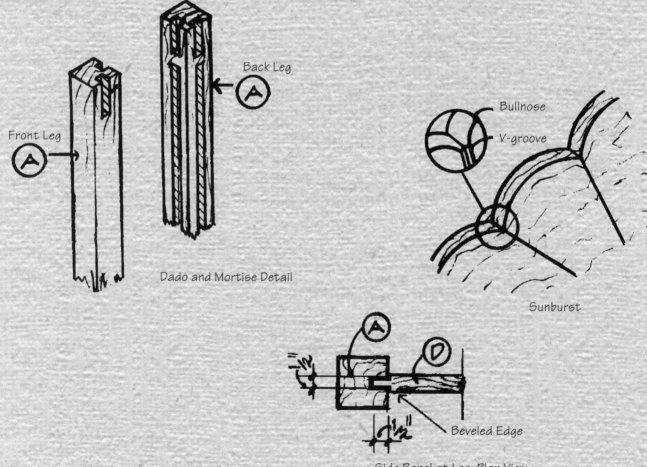

Front Leg   Back Leg

Dado and Mortise Detail

Bullnose

V-groove

Sunburst

Beveled Edge

Side Panel at Leg: Plan View

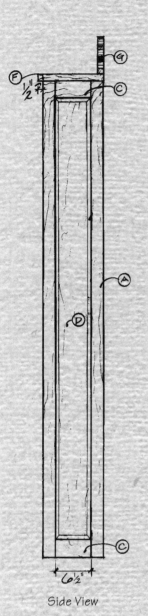

Side View

Creating the Corner Sunbursts

Carve two corner sunbursts (see Design Details of the Overview section for directions) and attach them to the underside of the top front rail with glue and dowels.

Assembling the Case

Slip a side panel into the dado of one leg (do not use glue). Put glue on the tenons of one pair of side rails (top and bottom), insert them into the leg mortises on one side, then fit the other leg onto the tenons of the rails. Clamp the panel assembly together until dry, and assemble the other side panel accordingly.

Put glue on the tenons of the back top and bottom rails and insert them into the mortises on one assembled side panel. Without using glue, slip the tongue-and-groove back panels into the dados. When complete, attach the other side panel to the back in the same manner.

Glue the tenons of the top and bottom front rails, and slip them into the mortises on the side panels.

Finally, make sure everything is square, then clamp the entire bookshelf together until dry. You can put a small dowel through the mortise-and-tenon joints for additional strength.

Installing the Shelves

First you need to drill ¼-inch holes, 2 inches apart, up the four inside corners of the case to hold the shelf support pegs. To do so, use a strip of pegboard as a template. The holes in the pegboard are already placed a convenient 1 inch apart.

Insert ¼-inch pegs to space the shelves as you wish. Cut the shelves to fit and lay them onto the pegs.

Attaching the Bottom and Top

Glue and screw ledgers around the inside of the top rails, flush with the top of the bookshelf. Fasten another set of ledgers around the inside of the bottom rails, set ¾ inch from the top edge. Cut a bottom panel to fit, place it onto the ledger strips, and screw up from the bottom of the ledgers into the bottom panel to hold it in place.

Cut out the top sunburst design according to the directions on page 82. Place it flush with the back of the top panel and screw up through the bottom of the top panel, to hold the sunburst in place. Then fasten the top onto the ledgers with screws from underneath. Allow for some overhang on both sides and in front.

NIGHTSTAND

Design

This nightstand is designed to accompany and complement the double bed and the *ropero*. Feel free to alter the decorative elements to complement your bed. There is a shelf inside to hold a phone book or other items, and plenty of room on top for your clock radio, lamp, and current reading. The dimensions shown may be altered in any direction to suit any specific use.

Making the Legs

Start by cutting out the four legs and marking the tops in some way so you know which ones are front and which are back, which left and which right. Cut a ¼-inch-deep by ⅜-inch-wide dado along the front and inside faces of each back leg and the inside faces of each front leg. Make sure to stop the dado about 2 inches short of the foot of each leg so it will not show beneath the bottom of the cabinet.

Cut ⅜-inch-deep by ⅜-inch-wide mortises at the tops of all eight inside faces of the legs to accept the four top rails. Cut similar mortises about 1½ inches up from the bottom of all eight inside faces of the legs, so the bottom rails will rest about 1½ inches off the floor (see illustration on page 95).

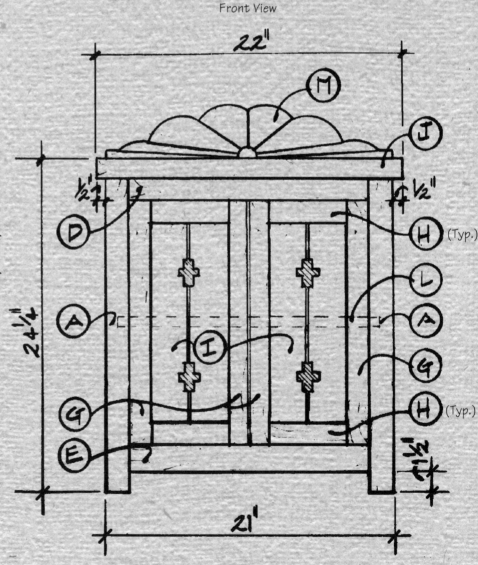

Front View

CUTTING LIST

Nightstand
(22" x 15" x 28¼")

Part	Qty	T	W	L	Piece
A	4	1½"	1½"	23"	Legs
B	2	1½"	1½"	13½"	Top Side Rails
C	2	1½"	2"	13½"	Bottom Side Rails
D	2	1½"	1½"	19½"	Top Rails (Front & Back)
E	2	1½"	2"	19½"	Bottom Rails (Front & Back)
F	11	¾"	4"❖	20½"	Side & Back Panels
G	4	1¼"	1½"	18"	Door Stiles
H	4	1¼"	1½"	6"	Door Rails
I	4	¾"	3½"❖	16"	Door Panels
J	1	1¼"	15½"	22"	Top
K	2	¾"	12"	18¾"	Floor & Shelf
L	1	¾"	1"	to fit	Ledger Material
M	1	1¼"	4"	21"	Sunburst

❖ Add ¼" to outside edges of outside panels to allow for tenons.

¼" Grid

Cross Pattern

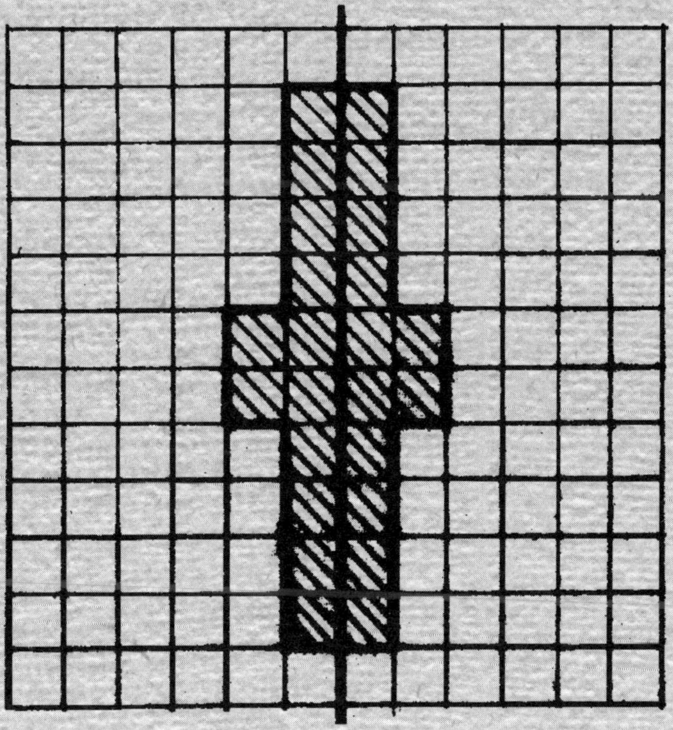

93

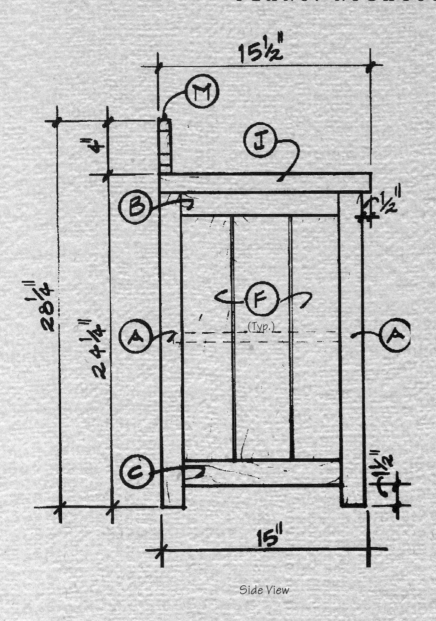

Side View

Assembling the Nightstand

Assemble the parts for both of the sides and the doors. Glue the mortise-and-tenon joints where the rails meet the stiles, but let the panels float in the dados without glue.

Put glue on the tenons of the back top and bottom rails and insert them into the mortises on one of the side panels. Using no glue, slip the back panels into the dados. Fasten the rails and back to the other side. Finally, glue the tenons on the front rails, and slip them into both of the sides. Make sure everything is square, and leave the nightstand in clamps until completely dry.

Installing the Top, Bottom, and Doors

Glue and screw ledger strips around the inside perimeter of the bottom rails, set ¾ inch below the top of the rail. Insert the bottom panel and fasten it in place by screwing up through the ledgers from below. Fasten two other ledgers halfway up the inside faces of the side panels to support the shelf, as shown above.

Cut out the sunburst pattern according to the instructions on page 82. Fasten it flush with the back edge of the nightstand top

Making the Rails and Stiles

Cut a ⅜-inch-long by ⅜-inch-thick tenon on each end of each rail (front, back, sides, top, bottom, and doors). Cut a full length ¼-inch dado along the inside face of each rail and stile.

Making the Panels

Cut a ¼-inch tenon on each end of each back and side panel and along the length of each outside edge of the door panels that slip into the stiles.

Clamp together the door panels that will be cut out with a negative space design. Lay out your pattern along the top edges (see the illustration on page 93), and cut away the material with a radial arm saw, saber saw, or back saw. Relieve all exposed sharp edges with a block plane or chisel. Cut slight bevels along the mating edges of the door and

side panels and along the tenons in the panels that slip into the rails and stiles to create a raised panel look.

PLANS: NIGHTSTAND

with screws inserted from underneath.

Glue and screw ledger strips around the top inside perimeter of the top rails, place the top onto the ledgers, and screw up into the top from underneath to hold it in place.

Finally, hang the two doors.

Back View

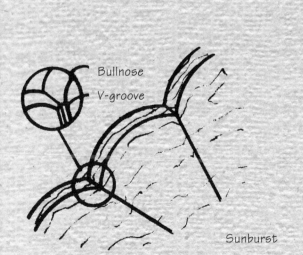

Bullnose

V-groove

Sunburst

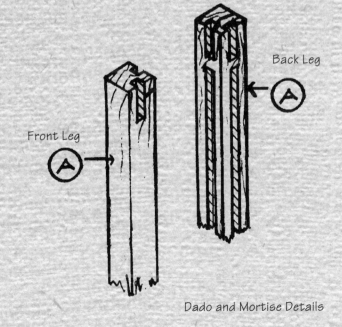

Back Leg

Front Leg

Dado and Mortise Details

95

ROPERO

Design

Traditional Spanish New Mexican cabinets fall into three categories. An *alacena* is a niche with wooden doors hung on pintel hinges that is built into the interior wall of an adobe house. A *trastero* is a standing cupboard divided horizontally into two sections, which often has doors top and bottom embellished with spindles or cutouts. A *ropero*, translated literally, is an individual who maintains the clerical wardrobe in a given community. However, the term is generally used to describe a free-standing clothes cabinet, also known as an *armario*. You could call it the New Mexican equivalent of the armoire or wardrobe.

The cutouts on this *ropero* are reminiscent of earlier designs that appear on cabinets traditionally used to store clerical vestments in a church. While the *ropero* is still used today for clothes, the addition of shelves also makes it useful as an entertainment center for a television set, VCR, and stereo.

This particular version was built overly large to accommodate a customer's set of wire-basket drawers. I made it so that it comes apart and can be moved through narrow doors or shipped flat. Its dimensions may be altered in any direction to suit a specific use.

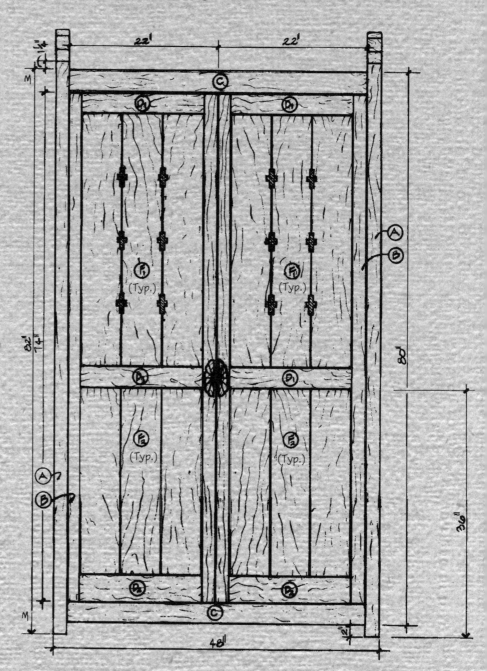

Front View

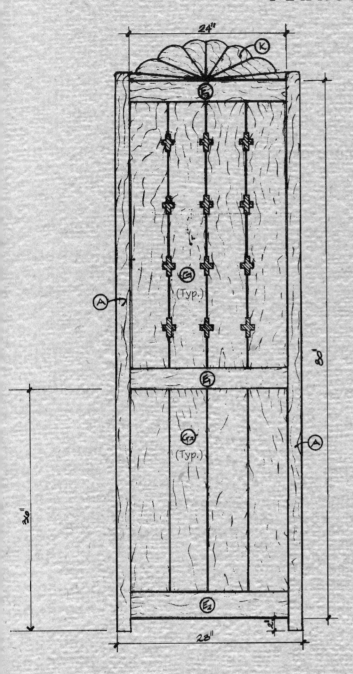

Side View

Making the Legs and Rails

Cut out the four legs and mark them left and right, front and back. Cut a ½-inch-deep by ⅜-inch-wide dado down the center of each of the eight inside faces of the front and back legs (see the illustration on page 100). Stop the dados about 2 inches from the bottom so the grooves will not show below the bottom edge of the cabinet. Cut the same dados into the facing edges of the back and side top and bottom rails. Also cut the same dados into the inside edges of the top and bottom door rails and the door stiles, and into both long edges of the middle back, side, and door rails.

Cut a ¼-inch-deep by ⅜-inch-wide mortise beginning 1¼ inch from the top of each of the eight inside leg faces to accept the four top rails, and a similar mortise 2 inches from the bottom of each of the eight inside leg faces so the four bottom rails will rest off the floor. Cut the same mortise into the inside faces of the legs to accept the middle side and back rails, and into each inside face of the door stiles to accept the middle door rails.

Cut a ¼-inch-long by ⅜-inch-thick tenon on the end of each rail.

Making the Side Panels and Doors

First, dry assemble the rails to the stiles (for both the case and the doors), and confirm the

97

exposed lengths of the door and side panels.

Next, cut a ½-inch-thick tenon along each end of each back, side, and door panel, and along the sides of the panels that will fit into the legs or stiles.

Clamp together the panels that will be cut out with a negative space design. Lay out your pattern (see the illustration on page 100) on the top edges, and cut away the material with a radial arm saw, saber saw, or back saw. Relieve all exposed sharp edges with a block plane. Cut bevels on the mating edges of the panels for a tongue-and-groove look, and bevel the outside edges of the panels along the tenons for a slightly raised panel look.

Assembling the Cabinet

Glue and assemble the parts for both sides, both doors, and the back. Let the panels "float" in their dados without glue.

With glue on the tenons of the top and bottom back rails, slip them into the mortises of one side panel, then slip in the back panels (use no glue). Fasten the other side to the back top and bottom rails in the same fashion.

Finally, glue the tenons of the front top and bottom rails into the side mortises. Make sure all is square, and leave in clamps to dry.

CUTTING LIST

Ropero
(48" x 28" x 88")

Part	Qty	T	W	L	Piece
A	4	2"	2"	83¼"	Legs
B	4	1¾"	2"	74"	Door Stiles
C	5	1¾"	3"	45½"	Front, Back, Top & Bottom Rails, & Mid-Rails
D1	4	1¾"	3"	19½"	Top & Middle Door Rails
D2	2	1¾"	4"	19½"	Bottom Door Rails
E1	4	1¾"	3"	25½"	Top & Middle Side Rails
E2	2	1¾"	4"	25½"	Bottom Side Rails
F1	6	¾"	6"❖	37½"	Top Door Panels
F2	6	¾"	6"❖	29½"	Bottom Door Panels
G1	8	¾"	6"❖	41½"	Top Side Panels
G2	8	¾"	6"❖	31½"	Bottom Side Panels
H1	8	¾"	6"❖	41"	Top Back Panels(T&G)
H2	8	¾"	6"❖	31"	Bottom Back Panels(T&G)
I	2	¾"	24"	44"	Top & Bottom
J	2 sets	1"	1"	to fit	Ledgers
K	2	1¾"	6"	25½"	Sunbursts

❖ Add ½" to outside edges of outside panels to allow for tenons.

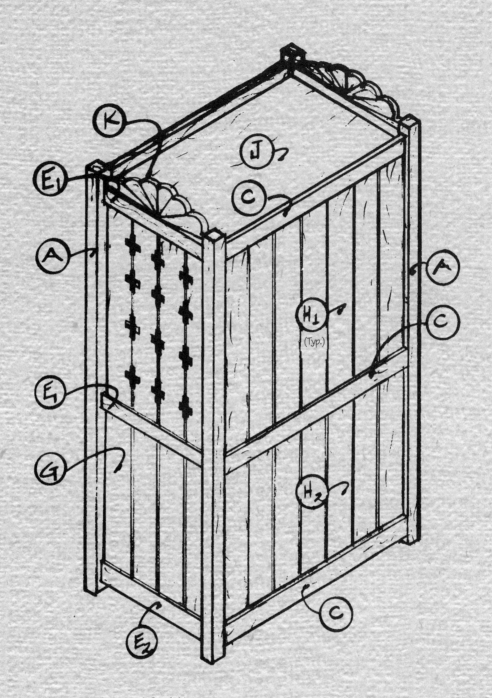

Side and Back View

Making the Top and Bottom Panels

Cut top and bottom panels to fit. Glue and screw ledger strips to the outside bottom edges of each, and screw them to the top and bottom rails.

Cut out sunburst patterns on two panels, according to the instructions on page 82. Then cut ½-inch-long by ⅜-inch-wide tenons onto the ends, so they slip into the dados in the legs which extend above the level of the top.

Completing the Doors

Carve door handles out of scrap material, drill holes, and screw them into place. Finally, hinge the doors to the front stiles.

(To make the *ropero* so it comes apart, clamp the front top and bottom rails and the back panel to the sides, and install hidden nut and bolt fasteners. If it does not need to come apart, fasten the rails and the back panel to the sides permanently.)

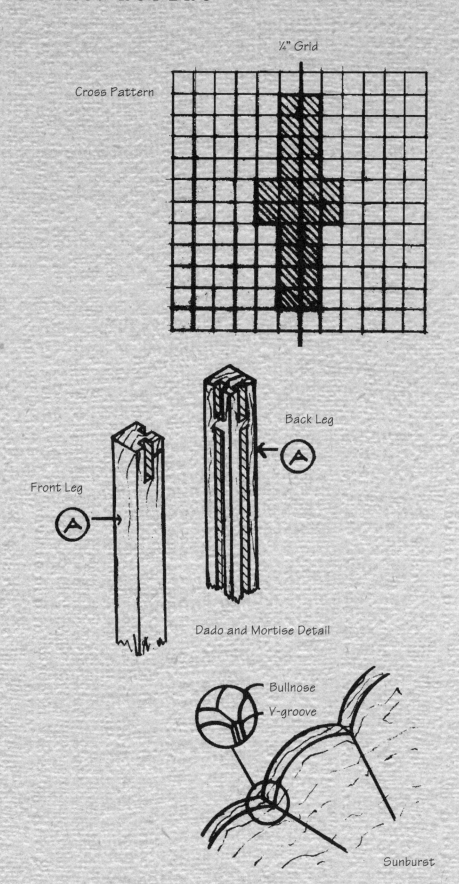

Cross Pattern

¼" Grid

Front Leg

Back Leg

Dado and Mortise Detail

Bullnose

V-groove

Sunburst

STANDARD DIMENSIONS
AND
GLOSSARY

STANDARD DIMENSIONS

*D*esigning and building your own furniture allows you tremendous leeway in producing pieces to serve your specific needs. There are, however, for many pieces, universally accepted dimensions that should be kept in mind, to ensure you produce pieces that are both functional and comfortable. These basic dimensions apply regardless of the style in which you are designing and building. They are offered here as a reference in order to save you furtive trips to the furniture store, armed with a tape measure and pad.

BEDS

When building a bed, add an inch or two beyond the size of the mattress to both the length and width, to give you room to tuck in blankets or quilts.

MATTRESS SIZES

Single (Twin)	39" x 75"
Double (Full)	54" x 75"
Queen	60" x 80"
King	76" x 80"

If your bed will not be used with a box spring, build it so the bottom edge of the side rail is 10 inches off the floor. If it will have a box spring, build it so the bottom edge of the side rail is 7 inches off the floor.

TABLES

Generally speaking, tables used for seating should stand between 29 and 30 inches off the floor. Since you need to allow a minimum of 6 inches from the top of the seat to the bottom of the apron, and since most seats stand about 17 inches off the floor, don't make the combined depth of the top and the apron greater than 7 inches.

Game, kitchen, and dining tables should be 29 inches to 30 inches high, and allow a minimum of 24 inches in width per person. A top 24 inches by 24 to 30 inches will seat two people; 36 inches by 36 inches will seat four; 40 inches by 60 inches will seat six; and 48 inches by 48 inches will seat eight.

A refectory table is a long dining table and should be a minimum of 27 to 48 inches wide, and as long as you like, allowing 24 inches per person.

Round dining tables should allow 20 to 24 inches of circumference per person. A diameter of 28 to 37 inches will seat four people; 35 to 45 inches, five people; 42 to 52 inches, six people;

49 to 60 inches, seven people; and 56 to 68 inches, eight people.

The top of an end table should be about even with the arm of the couch or chair next to which it will sit, or about 22 to 24 inches high.

A coffee table should be level with or just below the top of the seat cushions of the couch, or approximately 16 to 18 inches high. It can be about 17 to 19 inches deep by 26 to 30 inches long. If it is round, make it 26 to 30 inches in diameter.

FOOTSTOOLS

A footstool, like a coffee table, should sit a little below the height of the chair or couch seat with which it will be used.

GLOSSARY OF NEW MEXICO FURNITURE TERMS

Alacena — A cupboard that is built into an adobe wall with doors hung on pintel hinges.

Armario — A free-standing cabinet with doors, used for storing clothes; a wardrobe or armoire.

Banco — A bench, either free-standing or built into an adobe wall.

Carpintero — A carpenter or wood joiner; one who builds furniture, windows, doors, or wood-framed houses.

Repisa — A small shelf which hangs on a wall.

Ropero — Literally, an individual who maintains a clerical wardrobe; also used interchangeably with armario.

Serrucho — A carpenter's saw with a handle.

Tarima — A low, backless bench or stool.

Trastero — A free-standing cabinet divided into upper and lower sections, often with doors that are embellished with spindles or cutouts.

Vara — A unit of measure roughly equivalent to one yard or 84 centimeters.

BIBLIOGRAPHY

Bunting, Bainbridge. *Early Architecture in New Mexico*. Albuquerque: University of New Mexico Press, 1976.

Dickey, Roland F. *New Mexico Village Arts*. Albuquerque: University of New Mexico Press, 1949.

Katz, Sali. *Hispanic Furniture: An American Collection from the Southwest*. Stamford, Conn.: Architectural Book Publishing, 1986.

Mather, Christine, and Sharon Woods. *Santa Fe Style*. New York: Rizzoli, 1986.

Nestor, Sarah. "The Native Market of the Spanish Colonial Furniture Bulletin." Santa Fe: The Colonial New Mexico Historical Foundation, 1978.

New Mexico State Board for Vocational Education. "Spanish Colonial Furniture Bulletin." Santa Fe: State Board for Vocational Education, 1933.

Taylor, Lonn, and Dessa Bokides. *Carpinteros and Cabinetmakers: Furniture Making in New Mexico, 1600-1900*. Santa Fe: Museum of International Folk Art, 1984.

————*New Mexican Furniture, 1600-1940: The Origins, Survival, and Revival of Furniture Making in the Hispanic Southwest*. Santa Fe: Museum of New Mexico Press, 1987.

Vedder, Alan C. *Furniture of Spanish New Mexico*. Santa Fe: Sunstone Press, 1977.

Warren, Nancy Hunter. *New Mexico Style: A Source Book of Traditional Architectural Details*. Santa Fe: Museum of New Mexico Press, 1986.

Williams, A.D. *Spanish Colonial Furniture*. Salt Lake City: Gibbs M. Smith, Inc., 1982.

Wroth, William, ed. *Furniture from the Hispanic Southwest*. Santa Fe: Ancient City Press, 1984.

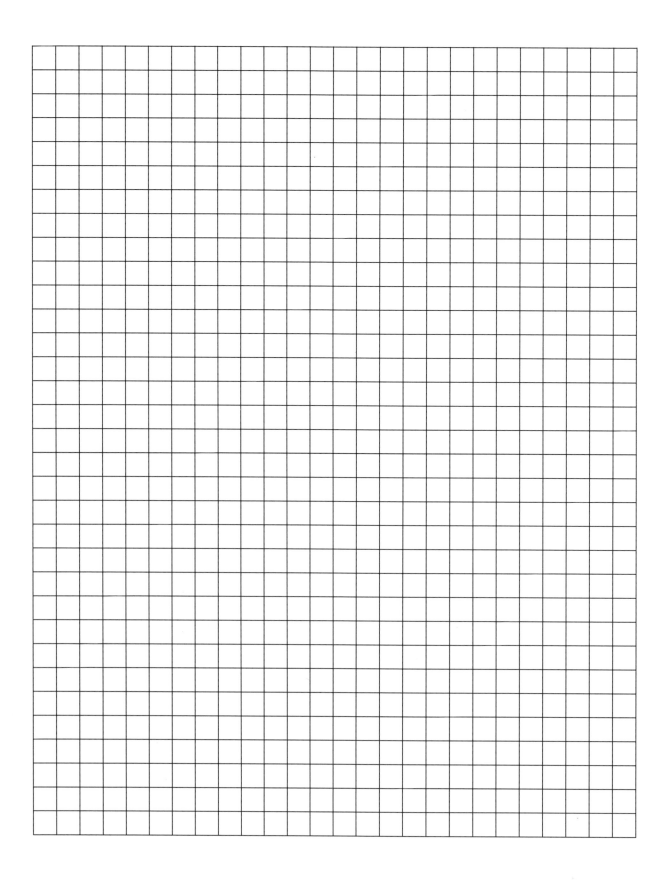

INDEX

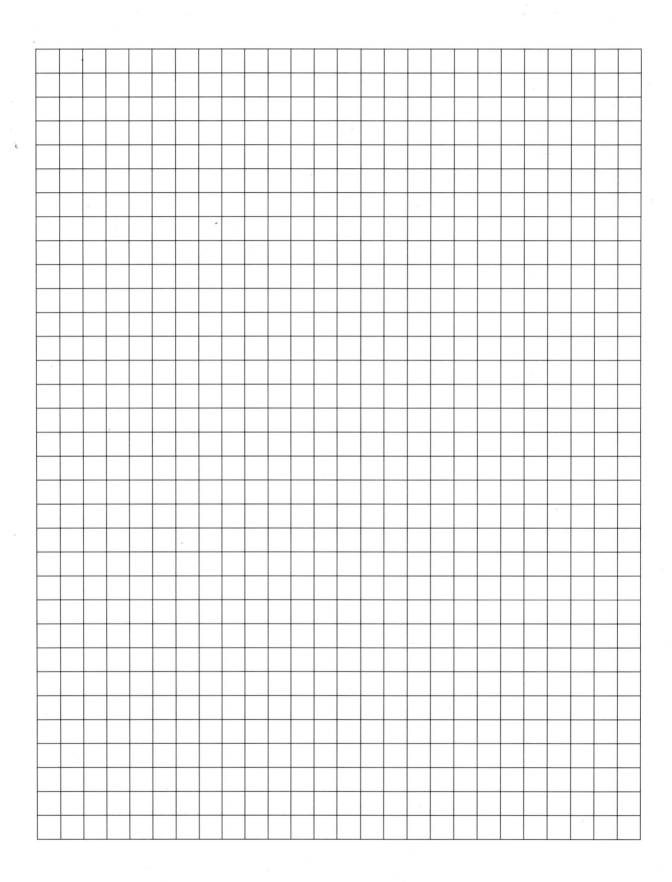